Jesus
The Storyteller

Relating His Stories to My Story

Brian L. Harbour

SMYTH&HELWYS
PUBLISHING, INCORPORATED • MACON, GEORGIA

Smyth & Helwys Publishing, Inc.
6316 Peake Road
Macon, Georgia 31210-3960
1-800-747-3016
©1999 by Smyth & Helwys Publishing
All right reserved.
Printed in the United States of America.

Brian L. Harbour

All biblical quotations are taken from the New Revised Standard
Version (NRSV) unless otherwise indicated.

Library of Congress Cataloging-in-Publication Data

Harbour, Brian L.
    Jesus the storyteller: relating his stories to my story/
    Brian L. Harbour.
    pp.   cm.
    Includes bibliographical references.
    1. Jesus Christ—Parables.
    2. Christian life—Baptist authors.
    I. Title.
    BT375.2.H27   1999
    242'.5—dc21   98-37032
                                                CIP
ISBN 1-57312-251-3

Contents

Foreword

Through the years I have had the privilege of reading several of Brian Harbour's books and also hearing him preach many times. Brian is not only theologically sound but he can take a complicated issue and give it popular expression without over-simplifying it. Further, I have always known Brian to be well prepared. In the more than 100 occasions I have heard him preach, I have never seen him enter the pulpit without extensive preparation. Brian is a communicator. He never adopted the more expressive oratorical styles of preaching, but he has established a style of communicating that is enthusiastic, upbeat, and warm without being religiously saccharine or rhetorically overblown. But perhaps what I have most appreciated about Harbour's preaching, and what this particular volume reveals as indicative of his own style, is his ability as a storyteller.

Storytelling involves at least two significant factors: the story and the telling of it. Brian understands and intuitively practices the nuances of rhythm, timing, inflection, and gesture. And he is a master in the difficult task of selecting and applying the story, which is the genius of this volume. Brian's intent is to introduce us to the parables of Jesus in all their evocative power. The strategy for achieving this goal is surprisingly successful inasmuch as it departs from the typical scholarly study of the parables found in any number of individual studies or commentaries. Nonetheless, Brian's chosen format is consistent with the character of the parables themselves, in that the parables are designed not only to teach illustratively in their historical settings, but also—both in the context of the life of Jesus and in the earliest contexts in the church—to elicit thought and a living response from the hearers.

Brian's format encourages us to reflect and to respond. He presents us with the given New Testament parable. Thus, we are immediately forced to do some interaction with the text. Then we are quickly, without commentary, thrown into a parallel world of story and illustration. Brian's technique is to place one or more additional stories and illustrations immediately before us and thus to create an imaginative connection—again without commentary—between the story Jesus told and the stories Harbour gives us.

Later on in the course of each individual study we are offered a few words of commentary, observation, and/or exhortation. But the real genius of Brian's presentation is his ability both to choose appropriate stories to lay alongside the parables of Jesus and his ability via the chosen format to force us to think about the parables of Jesus in ways that draw out our own interpretive skills.

I agree with many of my colleagues in preaching who say that, after the hard biblical homework is done, the most difficult task is finding the appropriate illustration. Of course, books of illustrations and/or humorous anecdotes abound as practical helps for preachers. But such stories not only lack personal warmth, but there is difficulty in seeing a connection between the story and a biblical text. How often speakers are reduced to having a great story to tell and no place to put it!

What Brian Harbour has done strikes a wonderful balance between spoon-feeding us and offering no connection. Again, what intrigues me most about this volume is not only the marvelous care with which the given stories were chosen—they range in type from the historically classical to the personal—but in the connections Brian implies with the New Testament parables. The result is not only a great resource for preaching, but particularly a provocative and devotionally rich resource for thinking. There is more than just good sermon stuff here; and there is more than just devotional exhortation. There is an opportunity for the reader to think creatively about the parables of Jesus and to offer other stories out of his or her own personal and devotional history to lay alongside the text. And, of course, we are challenged to respond in greater, more obedient faithfulness. This volume may be Brian's best yet.

—Robert B. Sloan, Jr.

Preface

Who is the best storyteller you have ever heard? Will Rogers was an American legend because he was able to tell a story. G. K. Chesterton became famous throughout England in the early part of the twentieth century because he could write a story. Mark Twain and Shakespeare, Og Mandino and C. S. Lewis—the list goes on and on. In a world of words where communication is crucial, the ability to tell a story that communicates truth is one of life's greatest gifts.

No one who ever lived could tell a story like Jesus. Two thousand years after his stories were told, these tales from the past continue to impact society with relevance, wisdom, and power.

The stories of Jesus are called "parables." The word parable comes from two Greek words: *para*, which means "alongside of," and *ballo*, which means "to throw." So a parable is a story thrown alongside a truth to illuminate it, to make its meaning clear. No one could do that better than Jesus.

Storytelling did not end with Jesus, of course, but has been a part of every generation since his time. Stories challenge, explain, probe, and amuse. They describe our lives and define our purpose, revealing who we are and who we long to be.

Stories are more popular today than ever. Books of heartwarming stories head the bestseller lists. Teachers of preaching talk about narrative preaching or preaching as story. Stories of murder and intrigue, relationships and conflict line the book racks at the checkout stands of grocery stores. People enjoy good stories.

In a day when people are hungry for stories, this book should have special appeal, not only because it focuses on the stories Jesus told, but also because dozens of other stories are wrapped around the stories of Jesus, giving different perspectives from which to approach his stories. The stories in this volume—both Jesus' stories and the others—can be remembered, retold, and shared by any person serious about Christian living today.

Debate has ensued through the centuries about the best title for Jesus. Should we refer to him as Lord or Christ or Son of Man or

Son of God? Which title is best? Maybe we need to remember Jesus as the Storyteller, one who threw common, real-life stories next to eternal, spiritual truths. And what lessons Jesus taught!

Why Winning the Lottery
Won't Make You Happy

Luke 12:13-21

At the age of 41, Bud should have been the happiest man alive, for he had won the first $2 million Georgia State Lottery. After telling the local media he would not change his lifestyle in any way, he went on a spending spree that included buying a new Corvette, a new house, and a whale-shaped swimming pool, and ordering 23 new credit cards with a total credit limit of $210,000. When he opened the envelope containing his first lottery check, he found a check for only $70,000. Only then did he realize what the limits of his new cash flow would be. Instead of happiness, he went into what psychonomists call "fiscal funk." [1]

Conversations are often punctuated with, "When I win the lottery, I'll . . ."—as if winning the lottery will instantaneously solve all our problems. Experience has taught us that winning the lottery often creates as many problems as it solves.

In an editorial he wrote about the lottery, Jerry Benson suggested that this warning be added to lottery tickets: "Accepting the proceeds from this wager can be harmful or fatal." He confessed in the article that he had often bought lottery tickets for all his enemies! He knew that winning the lottery would wreck their lives. [2]

Why do we seek so diligently for more money only to discover, when we get it, that money is not the answer? Jesus provided some insight on this dilemma in one of his most famous stories, the story of the fortunate but foolish farmer.

Farming is a risky occupation, the success of it determined by a number of factors. Some years everything comes together in just the right way, and a bountiful crop is produced. The farmer in Jesus' story had that kind of year. In fact, the crop was so plentiful, he had no place to store it. He needed new barns. Unfortunately, the farmer attributed to his vocational success more value than it actually had. He was convinced his future was secure. "Take life easy," he said to himself. "Eat, drink, and be merry." Or, in the words of Clarence Jordan, he said to himself: "Recline, dine, wine, and shine!"[3] But he didn't have a long life of leisure ahead of him. Instead, his life was over that night. He thought he had it made, but God called him a fool! What lessons can we learn from this remarkable story?

Money Can't Provide Fulfillment

Sister Priscilla of the Pristine Chapel was driving through central Texas. Just outside the town of Temple, on US 190 to Cameron, she ran out of gas. She walked back to a service station to buy some gas. The attendant at the station did not have a can to loan, so he took a 2-liter Dr. Pepper out of the refrigerator, poured out the Dr. Pepper, and filled the bottle with gas. When Sister Priscilla walked back to the car, she poured the gas into the tank out of the bottle. A passing motorist observed the scene, slowed down, rolled down his window, and said to the nun, "I admire your faith, Sister, but I don't think it's going to work!"

Just as the automobile was not made to operate on Dr. Pepper, we humans were not made to operate on money. This does not mean that money has no value; it does. It simply means that money is the wrong kind of currency for doing business in the spiritual dimension of life.

Suppose, for example, a businesswoman from Mexico City visits Dallas. She goes to the Galleria Mall to browse. In one of the stores she finds a beautiful vase. She decides to buy it. She takes the vase to the salesperson and hands him 2,000 pesos. He says to her, "I'm sorry, but those pesos are not good here." In Mexico, the pesos are worth something, but they are not the right currency for doing business in American stores. Likewise, money is not the right currency for buying fulfillment in life. Money can buy food, but not an appetite; medicine, but not health; acquaintances, but not friends; servants, but not loyalty; some days of joy, but not happiness.

Money, which is material, cannot satisfy our deep life needs, which are spiritual. Happiness comes only when we have peace with God, when we are at peace with ourselves, and when we live in peace with other people. Money simply cannot provide those things. That's why Jesus said in the introduction to his story, "For one's life does not consist in the abundance of possessions" (v. 15). Multiplying money to infinity changes the quantity of the money but not its quality. Five million dollars cannot bring fulfillment to human life any more than five dollars. Money simply does not have the capacity to provide fulfillment.

If we win the lottery, we may be rich, famous, and powerful, but we will not necessarily be happy. Happiness comes from a sense of fulfillment in life, and fulfillment is something money cannot provide.

The Desire for Money Controls Our Lives

Jethro, a wealthy silversmith, and his wife Josephine needed to journey at once to the city of Pulaski, about fifteen miles away. Because of snowfall the night before, the only available train was indefinitely delayed. Jethro approached a man named Theodore who had a coach and asked him to drive him and his wife to Pulaski. "The roads are covered with ice," Theodore protested. "In some places the snow is banked in ten-foot drifts. It is bitter cold. My horses may slip and fall. I will not do it."

Jethro countered this list of protests with another offer: "Take me to Pulaski. If I utter one sound during the entire trip, I'll pay twice the fare. But if I remain absolutely silent, then I owe you nothing."

Theodore considered the offer and decided to accept. "By the time I get him there," Theodore whispered to himself,

"He'll not only make a sound. He'll be hollering at the top of his lungs."

Theodore set out with his two passengers. He pushed the horses to full speed, reining them from one side of the road to the other, causing the coach to careen wildly. They hit every rock and bounced over every rut and hole, but not a sound came from Jethro. Finally, in desperation, Theodore raced the horses at the very edge of the road where the slightest mishap would send them plunging down the embankment. Jethro never broke his silence.

When they arrived at Pulaski, Theodore said, "You never made a sound. You win."

Jethro responded, "Just between you and me, I want to confess something. Back there at the last wild turn when the carriage nearly turned over, you almost won your bet. That's where my wife fell out!"

We can easily come to the place where Jethro was, caring so much about money that we don't care about anything else. We think we have money, but in reality, the money has us. That's the way it was for the fortunate but foolish farmer. Money controlled his thoughts. "What shall I do with all my abundance?" he asked himself. Money governed his plans. "I'll build bigger barns," he gloated. Money dominated his future. "I'll enjoy my abundance," he suggested to himself. The farmer thought he had all these material possessions, but in reality, they had him.

We, too, are often controlled by our possessions. We buy a boat and eventually go out every weekend on the lake and neglect our involvement in the life of the church. We think we have the boat, but in reality, it has us. We purchase a lake house, just to get away from some of the pressures in our lives. Soon we are going to the lake house every weekend and missing the weekly experiences of worship with God's people. We think we have a lake house, but in reality, it has us.

We often speak of money as a neutral force. It isn't. Richard Foster correctly concludes, "Money is not just a neutral medium of exchange but a 'power' with a life of its own. And very often it is a 'power' that is demonic in character."[4] That's why Jesus said, "Take care! Be on your guard against all kinds of greed" (v. 15). Money does not bring satisfaction; rather, it creates dissatisfaction. It produces an insatiable appetite, a desire for more, which eventually takes control of our lives.

Money Is Not Eternal

In 1886, some of the East Coast's most prominent millionaires—including Goodyear, Rockefeller, Vanderbilt, Morgan, Macy, and Astor—purchased a coastal island near Georgia for a winter family retreat. By the early 1900s, those men had informally linked together to form a powerful and influential confederacy. Members of the exclusive Jekyll Island Club controlled 1/6 of the world's wealth. Today the Jekyll Island Club is history. Those powerbrokers are all dead. When they died, without exception, they left their money behind.[5]

This real-life story is a parable that highlights the most dangerous aspect of money. Money and the things money can buy seem to offer security and permanency when, in reality, material things are temporary and transient. This truth is beautifully exposed in Jesus' story. Notice the sharp contrast between the farmer's illusion of "many years" (v. 19) and the reality of "this very night your life is being demanded of you" (v. 20). Centuries later, money still is limited by its temporary quality.

As family and friends gathered at the cemetery for the burial of the town's wealthiest citizen, one of the mourners said, "I wonder how much money he left." Another of the mourners responded, "All of it!" Of course, the dead man left all of it, and so do we. We *all* leave *all* of it, because the power of material things is only operative within the parentheses of the womb and the tomb. Money belongs to the realm of the temporary and transient.

Conclusion

The farmer sought money without recognizing its obvious shortcomings. Money cannot provide fulfillment, produce satisfaction, or procure permanence. That's why Jesus called the farmer a fool. He let go of the one thing he could keep, and he kept the one thing he should have let go.

People of our day share a kindred spirit with the farmer in Jesus' story. Sociologist Juliet B. Schor confirms that throughout the 1980s and 1990s, most middle-class Americans were acquiring at a greater rate than any previous generation. During that period the average American's spending increased 30 percent.[6] Is it possible that the intensification of our consumption is driven by the same motive Jesus discovered in the farmer, the illusion that the possession of things will allay our insecurities and affirm our worth? A popular bumper sticker puts it like this: "The one who dies with the most toys wins!" Jesus' story needs to make the rounds again today.

I once heard Dale Evans make a statement that provides a clearer focus than the distorted view of the fortunate but foolish farmer and the conspicuous consumers of our day. She said, "All my life I searched for a pot of gold at the end of the rainbow, and I found it at the foot of the cross." We, too, can find a pot of gold, not in the lottery, but in the "boundless riches of Christ" (Eph 3:8).

Notes

[1]Jerry Benson, "Pennies from Hell," *Omni* (June 1991): 112.

[2]Ibid.

[3]Clarence Jordan, *The Cotton Patch Version of Luke and Acts* (Clinton NJ: New Win Publishing, 1969) 53.

[4]Richard J. Foster, *Money, Sex, & Power* (San Francisco: Harper and Row, 1985) 24-25.

[5]Patrick M. Morley, *Walking with Christ in the Details of Life* (Nashville: Thomas Nelson Publishers, 1992) 7-8.

[6]Juliet B. Schor, *The Overspent American* (New York: Basic Books, 1998) 11-12.

The Kind of Religion
That Makes God Sick

Luke 18:9-14

*An inmate appeared in the courtroom of Judge Fred Axley,
Criminal Court Judge in Shelby County, Tennessee, to ask for
an early release from prison. When the judge asked him the
reason for an early release, the inmate said he had "found religion." After considering all the information, Judge Axley
refused the prisoner's request, explaining that his request was
premature. The inmate was then led away by the deputy sheriff. When the deputy sheriff returned to the courtroom, he was
laughing. "What's so funny?" Judge Axley asked. The deputy
sheriff explained, "I think that feller who said he had found
religion just lost it. You shoulda heard what he called you out
in the hall."*

That's one kind of religion that makes God sick, a religion that
presents a charade of goodness behind which an evil heart lies.
Jesus addressed this kind of religion in the Sermon on the Mount
when he said, "On that day many will say to me, 'Lord, Lord, did
we not prophesy in your name, and cast out demons in your name,
and do many deeds of power in your name?' Then I will declare to
them, 'I never knew you; go away from me, you evildoers' " (Matt
7:22-23).

Another kind of religion that makes God sick is religion that is
outwardly good, one that follows all the rules and does what is
right, but all for the wrong reason and with the wrong spirit. It is
this kind of religion that comes under the spotlight of the Storyteller's penetrating scrutiny in the story of the pointlessly proud
Pharisee.

Two men went to church one day. Mr. Pharisee sat on the front
row where everyone could see him. When he was called on to give
the invocation, what a prayer Mr. Pharisee prayed. He said, "God,
I am so thankful you have someone as wonderful as I am who
believes in you." Then he reminded God why he was so wonderful.
"I'm not like other people who do things wrong." He even made a
list of things others did that he did not do: "I don't take things

from other people. I don't treat people badly. I don't commit adultery. I don't take advantage of people." Then he listed things he did that others failed to do: "I fast twice a week. I pay my tithe. I follow the rules." The Pharisee said, "I am an outstanding person, and you should be thankful I take my time to worship you."

Bright, successful, disciplined—Mr. Pharisee was definitely religious. But Jesus said that the worshiper who simply prayed, "God, be merciful to me, a sinner" went home justified, whereas the Pharisee did not. The religion of the Pharisee did not please God. It was a religion that made God sick.

Religion still comes in many sizes and shapes. But not every expression of religion is genuine. Not every expression of religion pleases God. In our day, as in Jesus' day, there is a kind of religion that makes God sick.

A Religion Impressed with Itself

Savanarola, the distinguished Florentine preacher of the fifteenth century, watched one day as an elderly woman worshiped at the statue of the Virgin Mary that stood in his city's great cathedral. The next day he saw the same woman on her knees before the Virgin Mary. As each day passed, he noticed the same woman coming each day to worship before the Blessed Mother. Savanarola said to one of his fellow priests, "Look how she reverences the Virgin Mother."

The other priest said, "Don't be deceived by what you see. Years ago an artist was commissioned to create a statue of Virgin Mary for the cathedral. He sought a young woman to pose as the model for his sculpture, a young, lovely, beautiful woman who had a mystical quality in her face. Her image inspired that statue. The woman who now worships the statue is the same one who served as its model years ago. Shortly after the statue was put in place, she began to visit and has continued to worship religiously ever since." [1]

This woman was not worshiping the Virgin Mother; she was worshiping herself! Likewise, the Pharisee in Jesus' story didn't go to church to praise God; he went to praise himself. Luke said, "He also told this parable to some *who trusted in themselves that they were righteous*" (v. 9, author's italics).

That's the way it often is with us. We're like little Jimmy who was sitting in the back seat when his father turned left at the intersection. The back door swung open. Jimmy escaped injury only because he held on firmly to the arm rest. That night, as his mother put Jimmy to bed, she said, "You need to thank God for saving your life today." Jimmy responded, "Why should I thank God? I'm the one who held on!"

How many times have we gone through a day without ever thinking about God? In effect, we are saying to God, "I don't need you. I'm adequate to take care of myself." How many times have we completed a task with a litany of self-congratulation? In effect, we are saying, "God, you didn't help me. I did this all myself." How often do we come before God impressed with who we are and what we have done? In effect, we are saying, "How fortunate you are, God, to have someone worship you as wonderful as I am."

God demands and expects an open, humble, receptive, grateful attitude. A religion impressed with itself makes God sick.

A Religion Based on Rules

A young missionary couple became so discouraged on the mission field that they gave up and went home. Their discouragement came from the other missionaries who criticized them for not being spiritual enough. Because this young couple loved peanut butter, they made arrangements for some to be sent to them. The other missionaries had concluded that a mark of this couple's spiritual maturity would be to give up peanut butter. They were so critical of the young missionary couple that the couple gave up and went home![2]

11

The veteran missionaries had adopted a religious system based on rules. When the new missionaries did not follow their rules, this young couple was judged to be unfit. The Pharisee in Jesus' story had a set of lists, too. These are the things a religious person does not do. These are the things a religious person does. He made a list, checked it twice, and used it to determine who was naughty or nice. The Pharisee had a religion based on rules.

This legalistic spirit still prevails in the church today. According to Charles Swindoll, if he had to make a list of the enemies of vital Christianity today, legalism would head the list.[3]

So what is wrong with a religion based on rules?

In a religion based on rules, the list of do's and don'ts is never complete. We can never develop enough rules to cover every situation. Such an approach to religion leads to judgmentalism. If we do not follow the list, we are deemed to be unfit and unrighteous. In addition, living under legalism takes the joy out of our faith. A religion of rules is movieless, danceless, tobaccoless, pokerless, and joyless!

The Christian faith is not about following rules. It is about being in a vital relationship with a living Christ. That's why a religion based on rules makes God sick.

A Religion That Shows Contempt for People

An ancient story tells of a beggar who went to Moses and asked for bread. Moses said, "Come into my tent, and you shall eat with me." When they sat down, with the bread before them, Moses paused to praise God. The beggar didn't offer thanks. Instead, he just started eating the food. Moses looked at him sternly and asked, "Why didn't you praise God?"

"Why should I praise God?" the beggar retorted. "What has He done for me? Why has He allowed me to be so poor?"

Moses was so angry that he picked up his staff, beat the beggar, and ran him out of his tent. When the beggar had gone, God said to Moses, "Moses, why didn't you feed the beggar, and why did you beat him?"

"Because he didn't praise you," explained Moses, feeling very righteous.

God replied, "Moses, the man has not praised me for twenty years, and he is still alive. He has not praised me because during all that time you have neglected him. He is alive only because I am less religious than you are and have not allowed him to perish. It seems to me that if I were as religious as you appear to be, there would be no one left alive on the earth!"

That was the problem with Mr. Pharisee. He was more religious than God! He thought so highly of himself that he, in turn, thought lowly of others. Mr. Pharisee trusted himself and "regarded others with contempt" (v. 9).

This often happens in the church today. We hear: "He doesn't believe exactly as we do; run him off. He doesn't say things the way we do; put him down. He doesn't have the same list of rules we do; censure him. He doesn't belong to our church; he must not be worth much."

Such conclusions are based on an improper understanding of discipleship. The distinguishing mark of a true disciple of Christ is not the rightness of our theology, nor the righteousness of our morality, nor the richness of our devotional life, nor the rigors of our churchmanship. The distinguishing mark of a true disciple of Christ is how much we love people. Jesus said, "By this everyone will know that you are my disciples, if you have love for one another" (John 13:35). If our religion shows contempt for people, it makes God sick.

Conclusion

Now here's the good news, the positive side of the issue. We can come to God just as we are. We don't have to be someone special; God will make us special. We don't have to go through life wondering if there are some rules we aren't following that disqualify us before God, or if there is some secret list of rules we don't know about. All we have to do is to live daily in an open, responsive relationship with the living Christ. Likewise, we don't have to determine whether other people are righteous before God. That's God's job. All we have to do is love them.

The life of faith does not have to be burdensome to us or repugnant to God. Instead, the life of faith can be the most exciting, joy-filled, rewarding life there is, not through religion but through a relationship with Christ.

Notes

[1]Tony Campolo, *Seven Deadly Sins* (Wheaton IL: Victor Books, 1989) 74.

[2]Charles Swindoll, *The Grace Awakening* (Dallas: Word Publishing, 1990) 93-94.

[3]Ibid., 77.

The Bigness of Smallness

Mark 4:30-32

The people of the little French village gathered for their annual harvest festival, a week of celebration and thanks. They brought their own food. In addition, each family brought a bottle of wine they had made and poured it into the community barrel. At the climax of the celebration the mayor opened the barrel and began the round of toasts. When he opened the spigot and tasted the first sip, he discovered it was pure water! How did that happen? Each family had brought water and saved their own wine at home. Each was sure that, in so large a barrel of wine, a little water would never be noticed.

Many of us are convinced that our little part won't make much difference in the world, that our meager efforts won't be missed. So we pass quietly through life, intimidated by the multi-talented people around us who seem to make such a difference in the world. We are so insignificant. Our efforts are so small. What difference can we possibly make in the world? The Storyteller addressed this need in his remarkable story about a small but significant seed.

The time was early in the ministry of Jesus. Twelve men had followed Jesus because they believed he was the special agent who would establish the kingdom of God on earth. They left their nets and tax books and families to follow Jesus. They had great expectations, but nothing much was happening. Their efforts seemed negligible. They were discouraged.

Jesus told the disciples a story, a brief tale about a mustard seed. The kingdom of God is like a mustard seed that when planted is smaller than all other seeds. Yet, from that infinitesimal seed comes a tree larger than all the garden plants, a tree that forms large branches the birds of the air can use to rest on and find shade from the sun.

Do you know how small a mustard seed is? It takes 725-760 mustard seeds to weigh 1 gram, and 28 grams add up to 1 ounce.

In other words, it takes more than 21,000 mustard seeds to weigh 1 ounce! That's small. Yet something as small as a mustard seed has tremendous potential.

The Storyteller was speaking specifically about the kingdom of God when he told this story. The kingdom of God, Jesus said, seems at times to be so small in size, so meager in effect. Nevertheless, it is the most powerful force on earth. Here is the practical application for us: Something potent can come from something as insignificant as a simple word, one person, or a solitary decision.

A Simple Word

One Saturday night a young grocery store clerk locked the door of the store and began to clean up so he could go home. Someone knocked on the door. It was an elderly woman, standing outside, rapping on the door window. "We're closed," he said.

The woman pleaded, "Please, I need a head of lettuce."

Reluctantly, the clerk opened the door and led her to the produce section. After about five minutes of inspecting every head of lettuce in the bin, she said to the clerk, "Actually, I only need half a head of lettuce. Would it be all right if I just bought half a head of lettuce?"

The clerk said, "I'll have to clear that with the store manager. I'll be right back."

He went into the manager's office and told the manager, "You won't believe this, but some stupid, idiotic, cranky old woman wants half a head of lettuce!"

Just as he finished this sentence, he glanced in the mirror behind the manager's desk and realized the woman was standing right behind him. Without missing a beat, he added, "Fortunately, we have this fine woman who will take the other half!"

Did the young grocery clerk recover from his word unfitly spoken? I'm not sure. Sometimes we can cover what we have said, but one thing we cannot do is recover the word. Once a word is uttered, it cannot be retrieved. Once out of the mouth, it cannot be reeled back in. It is set free to make its impact, for good or for bad. And sometimes it is just a simple word.

Picture a young man named Billy, just hanging out with his buddies on a Saturday night. One of the guys looks around, and then turns to Billy and pats his pocket. "I've got some good stuff in here," he says. "Pure as driven snow and a lot more fun. Are you interested?" Billy says, "No!" Just a simple word, but how important that word is.

Picture a bright young couple on a Saturday evening in June. Gathered around them are all the people they love the most. Nearby are the families who nourished them. Standing before them is their pastor. "Do you take this man to be your husband?" the pastor asks. The bride says, "I do." Such simple words, but how important those words are.

Picture a twenty-year-old man named John. He also has gathered around him the people he loves the most and the family that nourished him. But the setting is entirely different from that of the young couple at the marriage altar. Instead of standing before a minister, he stands before a judge. Instead of getting married, he is on trial. The trial has been completed, the final statements of the lawyers have been given, and the jury has returned with its verdict. The judge reviews the verdict and asks John to stand. "How do you find the defendant?" the judge inquires. The foreman of the jury says, "Guilty!" A simple word, but how important that word is.

There are no unimportant words. Every word we speak takes on a life of its own and, for better or worse, makes its impact on the world. Therefore, we should exercise control of our tongues. A simple word has tremendous power!

One Person

A little girl about five years old strolled along the midway at the state fair of Texas. She held in her hand a fluffy pile of cotton candy that was about as big as she was. The humorous picture of such a little person attempting to eat something so big caught the eye of a man passing by. He said to the little girl, "How can a little girl like you eat all of that candy?" Without a moment's hesitation, the little girl answered, "It's easy, Mister. You see, I'm really much bigger on the inside than I am on the outside."

What a great truth to discover about ourselves! We are bigger on the inside than on the outside. How much better to feel like this little girl than to feel like the women pictured in a cartoon who were standing next to a sign that read, "The Low Self-Esteem Glee Club," and singing, "If you're worthless and you know it, say 'amen!'"

Many people today are singing that song, and saying "amen" with great gusto! They feel worthless. They don't believe they can make a difference in the world. We need to realize that we are bigger on the inside than on the outside. When we think only in terms of numbers and end up in the inferiority complex of the minority, we need to remember the potency of just one person.

Charles Wesley was only one person, and what's worse, he had to live under the shadow of his more popular brother, John. Still, two hundred years after he died, Christians all over the world are singing Charles' hymns.

Ethel Andrus was just one person, but at the age of 72 she started an organization that in half a century has become one of the most powerful lobbying forces in America, the American Association of Retired Persons (AARP).[1]

Candy Lightener was just one person. However, after her 13-year-old daughter was killed by a drunk driver, she gathered together a group of housewives. Those women held their first press conference less than 20 years ago. Since that time 1,000 new anti-drunk driving laws have been put on the law books. Worldwide there are 400 chapters of women working under the title of MADD—Mothers Against Drunk Driving.[2]

Every significant accomplishment in life started the same way, with one person who conceived an idea, one person who started a movement that eventually involved others. There are no unimportant people. Every person, no matter how small or seemingly insignificant, can make a difference in this world. We should demonstrate confidence in our living. Just one person has tremendous power!

A Solitary Decision

As a senior at Alvin High School, Nolan Ryan actually liked to play basketball more than baseball. He had dreams of playing basketball in college. When San Jacinto Junior College held a basketball tryout, Ryan wanted to go. But he had a problem. He was scheduled to pitch for his high school baseball team on the day of the basketball tryout. What would he do? He had to make a decision.

Nolan Ryan decided not to go to the tryout, to pitch instead. One of his friends decided to go to the tryout and as a result was declared ineligible to finish the baseball season.[3]

Every decision has consequences. Sometimes the consequences are bad. On other occasions they are good, as they were for Nolan Ryan, Hall-of-Fame baseball pitcher. What if Nolan had gone to the tryout? What if he had missed his senior year in high school baseball? Such a seemingly minor decision, but from it came awesome consequences.

19

There are no minor decisions. Every decision we make opens some doors and closes other doors and eternally alters the direction of our lives. We need to be careful about our decisions. A solitary decision has tremendous power!

Conclusion

There are no unimportant words. There are no insignificant people. There are no minor decisions. They are all pregnant with potential. That's why controlling our tongues is important.

"Look before you leap" is a well-known adage. We can paraphrase it to say, "Think before you speak!" If we think before we speak, we will say the *right word*—a word of encouragement to the depressed and a word of warning to the proud. If we think before we speak, we will say the right word at the *right time*—when it will be heard, when it will help. If we think before we speak, we will say the right word at the right time for the *right reason*—to build up instead of tear down, to give hope instead of despair. There are no unimportant words.

And there are no insignificant people. That's why demonstrating confidence in our living is important. No one else in the world —present, past, or future—is exactly like us. God made us that way. God planted a unique combination of gifts in our lives to enable us to accomplish a unique purpose. There are no insignificant people.

And there are no minor decisions. That's why we must be careful about the decisions we make. Every choice has consequences, and those consequences determine what choices will be available in the future. A decision to take the left fork in the road instead of the right fork will lead us to a totally different destination. Likewise, the seemingly simple choices of our lives can make a difference in where we end up and what we become.

Something potent can come from something as insignificant as a simple word, one person, a solitary decision, or a mustard seed!

Notes

[1]Harold Ivan Smith, *A Singular Devotion* (Old Tappan NJ: Fleming H. Revell, 1990) 233-34.

[2]A. L. Williams, *All You Can Do Is All You Can Do, But All You Can Do Is Enough!* (New York: Ivy Books, 1988) 127-29

[3]Nolan Ryan and Harvey Frommer, *Throwing Heat* (New York: Doubleday, 1988) 15-16.

What the World Needs Now

Luke 10:25-37

A Chinese woman's only son died. In great anguish she went to a holy man. "What magical incantations do you have to bring my son back to life?" she asked.

He answered her question with a request. "Fetch me a mustard seed from a home that has never known sorrow, and we will use the seed to drive the sorrow out of your life."

The woman set off at once in search of such a mustard seed. She came first to the mansion of an obviously wealthy family. "Surely," she said to herself, "this is a home that has never known sorrow." She knocked on the door and was greeted by a woman whose face revealed long nights of endless tears.

"I'm looking for a home that has never known sorrow," the visitor said.

"You've come to the wrong house," responded the matron, "for I have just gone through a terrible sorrow. Come in, and I'll tell you about it."

As they conversed, the visitor learned that the other woman had also lost a son. So she stayed to comfort her.

Soon the visitor continued her search for a home that had never known sorrow. Wherever she went, in mansions or in hovels, she discovered one experience after another of sadness and misfortune. She eventually became so involved in ministering to the grief of others that she forgot her own sorrow.[1]

There is no home without sorrow, no person without a problem. Joseph Parker of City Temple Church in London used to say, "Every pew has at least one broken heart."[2] A modern-day quip suggests: "Everyone either has a problem, is a problem, or lives with one!" Every person we meet has a burden, a problem, or a hurt. That's why the greatest need in our world today is people who care about other people. We need compassionate people.

What is compassion? Jesus provided some insight in his story of the spurned but sympathetic Samaritan. "The Good Samaritan," the title by which this story is commonly known, is an oxymoron. To the first-century Jew, the words "good" and "Samaritan" did not go together. It was like calling someone a smart idiot, or a tall dwarf, or a small giant. The words did not fit. Perhaps the most striking thing about the story is that Jesus used a hated Samaritan as the hero.

Why was the Samaritan a hero? Why do we call him good? He was "the Good Samaritan" because he demonstrated in his life the one thing that will bring relief to hurting humanity: compassion. As we study the response of the Samaritan in contrast to the other two characters in the story, we will understand what is involved in compassion.

Compassion Begins with Identification

Manual of Milwaukee faced one of the most feared afflictions of our day: cancer. When the chemotherapy treatment caused his hair to fall out in patches, he shaved his head. He was very self-conscious and worried about what his friends would think. His brother Julio learned how upset he was about his appearance. Guess what Julio did? He shaved his own head and persuaded fifty neighbors and relatives to do the same thing, and then the whole bunch went to the hospital to pay Manual a visit. It looked like a bald-headed convention![3]

When Julio wanted to show compassion for his brother, he chose to identify with his condition. Identification is the beginning point of compassion. See how this is spelled out in the story of the Good Samaritan. The story opens with the spotlight on a man in need. He is not identified. We don't know his nationality or occupation or if he had a family. He had been robbed, beaten, and left for dead. Three people walked by the man in need: a priest, a Levite, and a Samaritan.

24

According to social standards of the day, the priest was at the top of the social ladder. He was an important person. Yet, for all his importance, or maybe because of his importance, he refused to respond to the man at the side of the road. He did not recognize the wounded man as a colleague, so he passed him by.

The Levite was a junior priest. He had some religious duties and carried some weight, but he was lower on the social totem pole than the priest. Jesus described the reaction of the Levite in slightly different terms than the reaction of the priest. The priest "saw him," but the Levite "came to the place and saw him" (vv. 31-32). Perhaps the Levite expressed curiosity or mild pity. Perhaps he paused and looked for a moment at the poor fellow. But he did not stop or help. He passed by.

Samaritans were at the bottom of the social totem pole, spurned by the Jews. One writer of the day put them beneath Jewish slaves, Israelites with a slight blemish, Israelites with a grave blemish, and Gentile slaves.[4] Yet this Samaritan stopped. He saw—and helped.

Why the different response of the Samaritan? I believe it was because he identified with the man in need. This does not mean the injured man was a Samaritan. We are not told that. However, like the Samaritans, he had been kicked around, and was considered a nuisance and a burden. Only the Samaritan identified with the broken, hurting man. Jesus described his response in these words: "When he saw him, he was moved with pity" (v. 33). That's where compassion begins. To be compassionate means to identify with the broken and hurting.

When we come to the place in our lives where we identify with those who hurt, then we have taken the first step toward compassion. Compassion begins when we realize that we are all together in our sinfulness, brokenness, and need. Compassion begins with identification.

Identification Produces Feeling

A little girl in a small town went to the store for her mother one day. She was gone for a rather long time. When she arrived back home, her mother asked her why it had taken her so long. She told her mother about a little girl who had fallen and broken her doll. "I stopped to help her," she announced.

The mother, wondering what she could have done to help the little girl fix her broken doll, asked, "Honey, how did you help her?"

The little girl replied, "I just sat down beside her and helped her cry."

The world is filled with heartless people, people who are indifferent to the needs of others. Compassion breaks out of the stranglehold of apathy with an expression of empathy. The Good Samaritan felt this compassion.

The Greek word for compassion carries the idea of a movement in or a stirring of our inward being. The Latin root of the English word compassion means "to suffer with." To have compassion means to feel with those who are broken and hurting.

In one of his books Henri Nouwen presented a powerful portrait of compassion. He wrote:

Compassion asks us to go where it hurts, to enter into places of pain, to share in brokenness, fear, confusion, and anguish. Compassion challenges us to cry out with those in misery, to mourn with those who are lonely, to weep with those in tears. Compassion requires us to be weak with the weak, vulnerable with the vulnerable, and powerless with the powerless. Compassion means full immersion in the condition of being human.[5]

Nouwen made it clear that compassion is more than just identification with those who hurt. We must actually become immersed in their lives.

When we can cry with the world, then we have taken another step toward compassion. Compassion goes beyond the recognition that we are all together in our sinfulness, brokenness, and need. Compassion leads us to feel what others feel.

Identification and Feeling Result in Action

In a certain church a problem was discussed at the deacons' meeting. A young man about age twenty who loved to come to church and sit on the front row had emotional problems and a physical deformity that made people shy away from him. He made strange grunting sounds and was constantly moving, disturbing those around him. What should they do, the deacons asked themselves. Should they ask his parents to keep the young man at home? Should they tell the ushers not to seat him? They left the issue undecided, agreeing to consider the matter again at the next meeting.

The next Sunday the deacons were surprised to see one of their group who was the CEO of a successful corporation walk in with the young man. He sat beside the boy and placed his arm around him. All through the service he tenderly cared for him. He did this every Sunday for two years until the boy died.

The deacons were stymied. They didn't know what to do, so they discussed the issue and then tabled it for later consideration. How like our churches today! We appoint committees. We do studies. We investigate. We study. We pray. We just don't act. But compassion demands the move from the passive to the active. Compassion means translating good intentions and sympathetic feelings into tangible actions.

Notice the action verbs that permeate the Scripture passage. The Samaritan came to the beaten man, poured oil and wine on his wounds and bandaged them up, put him on his own beast, took him to an inn, and made arrangements for his care. Jesus condemned the priest and the Levite, not just because they did not identify with the injured man, not just because they did not feel anything for him, but primarily because they did nothing. They left the broken man at the side of the road to die. Compassion always results in action.

Compassion is something you do. It does not have to be something spectacular or expensive—sometimes just a word, or a smile, or the willingness to see someone through. When we allow our identification with and our feelings for the broken and hurting to propel us into action on their behalf, then we are demonstrating true Christian compassion.

Conclusion

All around us are people who are hurting, lonely, guilty, rejected, depressed, and afraid. Jesus' story is a perpetual reminder that these are the very people we are to love.

Why is compassion so important? Why should we love as Christians? In his epistle John presented the answers, and they are duplicated throughout the New Testament. We should love others because God first loved us. "Beloved," John wrote, "since God loved us so much, we also ought to love one another" (1 John 4:11). In addition, we should love others because our love provides a window through which the world can see God (v. 12).

There is an amazing parallel between this passage in John's first epistle and a passage in the prologue to his Gospel. The verses are tied together with the phrase: "No one has ever seen God."

No one has ever seen God. It is God the only Son, who is close to the Father's heart, who has made him known. (John 1:18)

No one has ever seen God; if we love one another, God lives in us, and his love is made complete in us. (1 John 4:12)

Just as the incarnation of Jesus reveals God to the world, the incarnation of God's love in us reveals God to the world.

Notes

[1]Harold S. Kushner, *When Bad Things Happen to Good People* (New York: Avon Books, 1981) 110-11.

[2]Andrew W. Blackwood, *The Growing Minister* (Grand Rapids: Baker Books House, 1960) 16.

[3]Maxie Dunnam, *Perceptions* (Wilmore KY: Bristol Books, 1990) 59.

[4]Peter Rhea Jones, *Studying the Parables of Jesus* (Macon GA: Smyth & Helwys, 1999) 307-308.

[5]Henri Nouwen, Donald P. McNeill, and Douglas A. Morrison, *Compassion: A Reflection on the Christian Life* (New York: Doubleday, 1982) 4.

You *Can* Go Home Again

Luke 15:11-32

One of America's exceptional novelists of the early twentieth century was Thomas Wolfe. His last novel, published after his death in 1938, is the one for which he is most widely known. This autobiographical sketch describes a haunting search for meaning in life. George Webber, the protagonist of the story, published a highly successful novel, followed by a second, but these did not bring a sense of fulfillment.

When he went back to his hometown of Libya Hill, George discovered that things were not the same. The greed of the town leaders repulsed him. He then went to Germany. He had always felt a kinship with the German people, but in 1936, they were far different from what he had known before. He returned to America, only to be disillusioned about the direction America was taking. His unfulfilled longing to rediscover the stability and peace of his past led George Webber to the conclusion that "You Can't Go Home Again"—the name of his novel.

Thomas Wolfe was wrong. No matter where we have gone or what we have done, we *can* go home again to the Heavenly Father. Jesus made that clear in probably his most unforgettable story, the story of the riotous but repentant rebel. Three characters move on and off the stage in this dramatic story.

First, there was the son who ran away. He demanded his inheritance and claimed his freedom. The descriptive word for this first actor in the story is *rebellion*. This son demonstrated the spirit of rebellion that has touched the heart of almost every person at one time or another.

The second character is the father who never gave up. He released to his rebellious son his inheritance, and he gave him his freedom. The descriptive word for this second actor in the story is *love*. When the rebellious son wanted to leave, the father was flexible. While the rebellious son was gone, the father was faithful. When the rebellious son wanted to come back home, the father was forgiving.

A third character enters the drama near the end of the story, the older brother who stayed home. Even though he stayed at home, he was not at home with his father. The descriptive word for the third actor in the story is *self-righteousness*.

This famous story has been labeled with different titles. Usually, we call it the story of the Prodigal Son because the young son who left home is the central figure of the drama.

Three questions are keys to the story: Where did he go? Why did he go? How did he get back home?

Where?

I once rode to a cemetery with a man whose mother we were burying. The cemetery was located next to the church where the man grew up. It was a journey of some distance, so we became involved in a long conversation. I asked him if he was a Christian. "Oh, yes," he said. "I've been a Christian since I was a boy." I asked him to share his story. He said, "When I was about ten years old, I took my stand for the Lord and was baptized in this little country church." That was his entire Christian testimony. When I asked him what had happened since then, he explained, "When the church closed several years ago, they sent me my church letter. I have it in a trunk in my attic. Someday I'm going to do something about it."

The prodigal son gathered all he had and took his journey into a "far country" (RSV). Where is the far country? The adjective "far" may confuse us. We think of the far country as being somewhere a great distance away, across the ocean, on the opposite side of the globe. Because the far country is such a great distance away, we think of it as being a place beyond our reach. The far country, however, is not a great distance away nor beyond our reach. It is very close and within the reach of every one of us. The far country is wherever a person lives without God.

The man with whom I had a dialogue as we traveled to his mother's funeral was obviously in the far country. We might be, too. We might still be at home. We might still be living in the same geographic area where we have lived all our lives. But if we are living there without God, we are in the far country.

We might be following the same routine we have followed for years, going to work at the same place, following the same route, coming home to the same house, going through the identical routine day after day, but if we are doing all of this without God, we are in the far country.

The far country is wherever we live without God. How do we know if we are living in the far country? If we are spiritually depleted, detached, or defeated, we are living in the far country.

Some Christians have constructed around their emotions a barricade of profound apathy that has dulled their spiritual senses. They have moved away from God and planted themselves in the far country. When all we can talk about in our relationship with God is something that happened a long time ago—an experience in our childhood, an encounter with God at an earlier age, a church where we used to be active—if we only have a past tense in the spiritual realm of our life, we are dwelling in the far country.

Many Christians have been loved by God, redeemed by Christ, and empowered by the Holy Spirit but are timid in their witnessing, afraid when facing problems, hesitant when they carry out Christian service, uncertain about what they believe, and pessimistic about the future of the church. They go through life without joy, exuberance, or enthusiasm. They have been made "more than conquerors" through Christ (Rom 8:37), but they are defeated by life.

When we limp through life from one defeat to another, when we accomplish nothing for God, when we live within the parameters of only what we can do, then we are in the far country. The far country can be right here, right now. The far country is wherever we try to live without God.

The Prodigal Son had everything he needed at home to live a full life. Instead, he chose to seek his fortune in a "far country."

Why?

In the days of Stalin's Russia, a Russian wolfhound left his native country and went to Paris where he became acquainted with a French poodle.

"Life is great under Communism," said the wolfhound. "I had an air-conditioned doghouse, plenty of juicy meat, and all the rabbits I wanted to chase."

The poodle asked, "Why, then, did you come to Paris?"

The wolfhound said, "I had an overpowering urge to bark for a few days."

Like the Russian wolfhound, we all have the desire for freedom, which we think will in turn bring happiness. This desire probably motivated the Prodigal Son. "If I can just get away from home and the authority of my father," he said, "then I will be free to do what I want to do." "It's boring around here," he whined. "I want to go where the action is."

Because we want freedom from the responsibilities of the Christian life, many of us turn away from God and end up in the far country. We believe happiness is more likely found in the arena of the world than by living in fellowship with God's people and in obedience to God's word. Often in search for this happiness, we turn away from God and end up in the far country.

Most of us do not end up in the far country because we desire freedom from God's rules nor because we are driven by a desire for the world's happiness. We are in the far country because we have drifted there. We didn't intend to go to the far country. We don't want to be there. Somewhere along the way we simply drifted away from our Father's house.

This drift can start when we take a little vacation from church or move to a new city, become too busy or get mad at God, or when we are newly married or disappointed about the church. Thousands of Christians who belong to churches all across the land began their Christian lives with the best intentions and professed their faith with the warmest sincerity. But then something happened. They put off their responsibility to God, began to drift away, slipped away from their Father's house, and ended up in the far country.

How?

A young lady in the neighborhood of my church had sent her child to our Mother's Day Out program. She was not a member of the church, so I wanted to find out more about her family. I went to her home for a visit. When I identified myself at the door, she invited me to come in. A few minutes later her husband came home from work. As he walked into the room, she stood up and said, "Honey, this is the pastor from Woodland Hills Baptist Church. He came to talk to you about God." Then she walked out of the room.

Rather awkwardly, we sat down and began to talk. It was as if a dam broke and all the desires and needs and hurts of his soul came pouring out: the story of his earlier involvement in church, his teenage rebellion, his haunting emptiness as an adult. When he had talked himself out, I shared with him how Christ could meet his need. We then kneeled in his living room as he gave his life to the Lord.

When it was time for me to leave, he grabbed me by the shoulders and pulled my face right up to his. "Preacher," he said, "I have been waiting five years for someone to help me get straightened out with God."

We don't know how many years the Prodigal Son waited for someone to help him get straightened out with God. Finally, he discovered the good news that we can go home again. How? The Prodigal demonstrates the steps for us: (1) Consider your life. (2) Change your attitude. (3) Return to God.

In the slop of the pig pen the Prodigal took a long hard look at himself, and he didn't like what he saw. The Bible says, "He came to himself" (v. 17), or as we may say, "He came to his senses."

A young lady was discussing with me the situation in her home. She said, "I'll just have to put it this way. Things are not as they should be." Looking at our lives and admitting that things are not as they should be is the first step in going back home.

The Prodigal said, "I will get up and go to my father, and I will say to him, 'Father, I have sinned against heaven and before you' " (v. 18). His attitude had certainly changed since the beginning of the story when he demanded his inheritance and headed for a good time in the big city. This young man came to the realization that not only was it wrong to be where he was, but also that it was right to be with his father. He remembered that the only life that had any meaning was life lived in fellowship with his father.

Driven by the hope of a forgiving father, the Prodigal left the pig pen and went back home. He didn't just think about what needed to be done. He didn't just talk about what needed to be done. He did it!

Conclusion

We can go home again because the father who waits for us there loves us. This truth forms the backdrop of this human drama played out in Luke 15. That's why some prefer to call this story the parable of the Loving Father. Let me give you two images.

Temple, Texas, 1958: I'm sitting behind the wheel of an automobile, ready to take my driving test. Seated in the passenger seat is a man with a clipboard and a pencil. He tells me to begin. I pull out into the lane. Tires screech. Horns blare. He writes something on his clipboard. He tells me to turn left at the corner. He forgets to tell me to stop at the stop sign. More tires screeching. More horns. Something else goes on the clipboard. It's time to parallel park. I can't parallel park. Couldn't then. Can't now. I hit the signs front and back. More notes on the clipboard. We finally return to where we started. He studies his notes and tells me I failed the test.

Dallas, Texas, 1978: I'm sitting behind the wheel of an automobile, leaving the Shiloh Terrace Baptist Church and heading for home. My daughter Cara, four years old, gives me a look that says, "I want to drive." So she slips over into my lap, and we turn onto La Prada on the way to the house. Her hands are on the wheel at the top. My hands are on the wheel at the bottom. I tell her when to use the turn signal. I help her as we make our turns. We pull up to the front of the house. I turn off the motor. I give her a hug and say, "Cara, you are a great driver!"

Some people understand God in terms of this first picture. God is the person with the clipboard and pencil, making marks every time we break a rule, determining if we are going to pass or fail.

The picture of God in this remarkable parable from the Storyteller is the second picture. God is the one in the driver's seat, the one in whose lap we're sitting, the one whose hands are on the bottom part of the steering wheel, the one who tells us when to use the turn signals, the one who helps us make the right turns.

Because God is for us and not against us, because God loves us, because God is waiting for us with open arms and a longing heart—we can go home again!

Get a Life!

Matthew 7:24-27

One of the greatest talents ever to play baseball was a Native American named Louis Sockalexis. He signed with the Cleveland Spiders in 1897. His first year he amazed the baseball world with his tremendous arm, his impressive speed, and his .331 batting average. Sockalexis made such an impact, his team changed its name from the Spiders to the Indians in honor of him.

Sockalexis was bright and well educated. He seemed to have a brilliant future. But it was not to be, for there was one opponent he could not beat, the opponent called alcohol. In a drunken stupor one night he jumped from the second floor of a brothel and broke his ankle.

That was the beginning of the downfall of Sockalexis. He eventually drifted back to his reservation. At age 42 he died alone in the woods, with old newspaper clippings about him stuffed inside his shirt.[1]

Sockalexis does not stand alone, but rather is one of a company of thousands who have demonstrated the tragedy of a wasted life.

In the Old Testament we see it in Solomon. At the beginning of his monarchy he was so much in tune with God that, when God offered to give him anything he wanted, the newly anointed king asked for wisdom. But eventually, the affluence and power of his position and the impact of his wives' many gods eroded his spiritual power and robbed him of the life God had planned for him.

In the New Testament character Demas we see the tragedy of a wasted life. At the beginning of his walk with Christ he was so much in tune with the kingdom, Paul described him as "my fellow worker" (Phlm 24). But eventually, the luster of discipleship was eclipsed by the lure of the world, and Paul wrote that Demas was "in love with this present world" and "deserted me" (2 Tim 4:10).

The spirit of Solomon and Demas—and Sockalexis—has reappeared in many of our contemporaries. They might go by the name of Tom, Dick, or Harriett, but they carry within them the spirit of Demas. Having been redeemed for life (see John 10:10), they live beneath their privileges.

How can we be sure this will not happen to us? The Storyteller provides some insight in his remarkable tale of the buffeted and besieged builders.

The Right Foundation

The builders of the 60-story Chase Manhattan Bank building discovered that the location had quicksand in it. They had a choice. They could move to another location, or they could build on another foundation.

The Chemical Soil Solidification Company sank pipes down to the quicksand and forced a solution of sodium silicate and calcium chloride through them. In just a few days the quicksand was changed to a solid and watertight sandstone that formed a wall to contain the quicksand and enable the construction to proceed.[2]

Two kinds of foundations are used in the construction of a building: spread foundations and pile foundations. Spread foundations are long slabs of concrete extending beyond the outer edges of the building that rest on the ground but are of sufficient size to spread the load over a wide area of the ground. Pile foundations are long slender columns of steel or concrete that pierce the earth for long distances to rest on bedrock.

The two buildings in Jesus' story reflect these two different kinds of foundations. The foolish man had a spread foundation, for his house rested on the ground. Unfortunately, the ground was sand that could easily erode. The wise man had a pile foundation, for his house rested on the bedrock. Fortunately, this provided a solid foundation that was not disturbed by the descending rains or robust winds or rising waters. The wise man built his house on the right foundation, but the foolish man did not.

We can choose the foundation on which we build our lives. If we build on money, we make a mistake because money isn't eternal. If we build on goodness, we make a mistake because goodness isn't sufficient. If we build on relationships, we make a mistake because relationships aren't permanent. If we build on physical health, we make a mistake because physical health isn't fixed.

The only firm foundation for life is the grace of God. The only way to experience the grace of God is by putting our lives in the hands of Jesus Christ through faith and acknowledging him as our Lord and Savior. To build a house—or a life—that lasts, we need to build on the right foundation.

The Right Material

A rich landowner approached his master carpenter one day and said, "I have plans for a lovely home on that beautiful hill. I want you to build the house. Employ the best workers. Use the best material. I want you to build a good house." Then the rich man went away on an extended trip.

The carpenter started on the house. As he proceeded, he decided to cut costs and pocket the difference. He built the house with inferior materials and the cheapest possible labor. The house was completed, the carpenter was richer, and, he thought, the owner would not know the difference.

When the rich owner returned, the carpenter told him the house was completed and that it was a good house. "Great," said the owner. "I'm glad it is a good house. My desire was to reward you for your years of faithful service to me. The house is for you. It is yours." 3

The right foundation is the place to begin building a life, but it is not enough. Upon the solid foundation we must build with the right material. What is the right material for building a life? Jesus tells us in the story. The wise man, the one who built a house that endured all the storms, is one who "hears these words of mine and acts on them" (v. 24).

Some people know what they need to do in life, but they don't do it. Others are action-oriented. They always do something, but they are not doing the right things. Hearing without acting has no value. Acting without hearing has no virtue. The key is to hear and act. The word that describes this combination of hearing and acting is the word obedience. The right building block with which to construct our lives is obedience, obedience to God's word and to God's way.

In God's challenge to the Old Testament people, blessing was promised "if you obey the commandments of the Lord your God," and a curse "if you disobey the commandments of the Lord your God" (Deut 11:26-28). In Christ's challenge to the New Testament people, obedience again was the key. Jesus said, "If you keep my commandments, you will abide in my love" (John 15:10). "You are my friends if you do what I command you" (15:14). The manifestation of the Son (14:21), the indwelling of the Father (14:23), the privilege of God's holy friendship (15:14), the power of prayer (15:16)—all of these are dependent upon our obedience. What does this mean?

We are to obey God now and always, not only at some future time or when it is convenient. We are to obey God in everything, not just in the significant things. We are to obey God wherever we are, not just at church. Obedience is the right material for building a life that lasts. We are to hear the word and do it.

The Right Ending

Pilot Howard Rutledge of the United States Air Force was shot down over Vietnam and spent several years in a prison camp. He describes the darkness and eventual light of that experience in his book, In the Presence of Mine Enemies. *In the utter helplessness of his experience Rutledge discovered how inadequate were the resources for life within him. He sank to the bottom and found nothing. A change in attitude and a transformation of spirit created a spiritual hunger within him. Without a pastor or Sunday School teacher or Bible or hymnbook, Rutledge began his search for God. He concluded, "It took prison to show me how empty life is without God."* [4]

For many Americans, Vietnam was more than just a topic to study in history class. It was a time of testing.

Jesus taught us that eventually every life will be tested. Storms come both to the wise builder and the foolish builder. These tests reveal what kind of life we have built. These tests are of two kinds: the daily tests that come in the experience of living and the final test that comes in the experience of dying.

The kind of life we build will determine the quality of our lives on earth and the quality of our lives after we leave this earth. If we build on the right foundation, and if we build with the right material, only then can we have the right ending.

Conclusion

Sometimes a single line in a movie brings together the entire story. *Braveheart*, the historic epic that describes the political turmoil in Scotland and England in the late 1200s and early 1300s, is like that. The movie describes the battle between Edward the Long-shanks, the perverse pagan king of England, who tries to take over Scotland, and William Wallace, the Scottish hero who will not sell his soul to the king. After a valiant effort, William Wallace is betrayed by one of his fellow Scots, resulting in his capture. On the night before he is to be tortured and put to death, a friend tries to persuade him to yield his allegiance to the king. Wallace says that to do so would make a lie of everything he is and everything he has done. "If you do not confess," the friend cries, "you will die." Wallace responds—and here's the line that defines the movie— "Every man must die, but not every man really lives."

Someone once said there are two important days in every person's life: (1) the day you were born and (2) the day you discover why you were born. I would add a third important day: the day you decide you are going to really live. Maybe today can be that important day for you!

Notes

[1]Daniel Okrent and Steve Wulf, *Baseball Anecdotes* (New York: Harper and Row, 1989) 35-36.

[2]Norman Vincent Peale, *This Incredible Century* (Wheaton IL: Tyndale House Publishers, 1991) 297-98.

[3]Lloyd John Ogilvie, *You've Got Charisma!* (Nashville: Abingdon Press, 1975) 151.

[4]Howard and Phyllis Rutledge, with Mel and Lyla White, *In the Presence of Mine Enemies* (Old Tappan NJ: Fleming H. Revell, 1973) 34.

When You Can't Be *the* Best,
Be *Your* Best

Matthew 25:14-30

The president of a company gathered all his employees together for an important announcement. Positioned in front of him were all the employees of the company. Standing beside him was an overalls-clad man off the assembly line.

"Ladies and Gentlemen," announced the president, "you are about to see how American industry rewards those who are conscientious and hard working. This young man standing beside me has been with the company less than a year. During that time his unusual qualities have earned him salary increases in excess of $200 a week. I have watched him closely and have been impressed with the manner in which he has done his work. Therefore, I am pleased to announce that starting this very afternoon, he gets off the assembly line and comes into the executive branch. He is now the executive vice president in charge of policy at an annual salary of $80,000." Turning to the young man, the president said, "Congratulations to you, sir."

The workman smiled, shook the extended hand of the president, and said, "Thanks, Dad."

Is success achieved in today's world through our connections? Connections are certainly important in our day of networking, but there is more to success in life than just knowing the right people. The Storyteller addressed this question of success in one of his most familiar tales, the story of the similar but separate servants.

A man had three servants. To each he gave some talents—to one he gave five, to another he gave two, and to another he gave one. (The word "talent" referred to an amount of money, but because of the phrase "each according to his own ability," the story of Jesus is usually understood as a reference to abilities.) After awhile the master returned and demanded an account from each servant as to how he had used his talent. The five-talent man had used his talents and gained five more. The two-talent man had used his talents and received two more. The one-talent man had hidden his talent. When the master returned, this servant had only the talent with which he began. To the first two servants, the master gave a word of commendation. To the third servant, the master gave a word of condemnation.

Today we don't call money "talents," nor are we the slaves of masters. Yet this story intersects our lives at the point of our accountability to God. It teaches us some important lessons about value and success.

Value

Dearest Papa,

I cannot write in verse, for I am no poet. I cannot arrange words and phrases artistically so as to produce effects of light and shade, for I am no painter. Even by signs and gestures I cannot express my thoughts and feelings, for I am no dancer. But I can do so through sounds, for I am a composer." [1]

This letter from young Mozart to his father reveals that he had a clear understanding of his own strengths and weaknesses. He could do some things well, but not everything. He was gifted in some areas, but not in every area. We often forget this truth about ourselves.

Thomas Jefferson penned one of the most sacred and significant of our American documents. We know it as the Declaration of Independence. The document begins, "We hold these truths to be self-evident, that all men are created equal." With all due respect to Thomas Jefferson, this simply is not true. Of course, Jefferson was referring to our equal rights as American citizens, but we have broadened his statement to mean equal endowment as individuals. Actually, we are not all equally endowed intellectually, physically, or emotionally.

President James A. Garfield could write with either hand. In fact, he could write Latin with one hand and Greek with the other hand—at the same time![2] Even if I learned Latin and boned up on my Greek, I could not write the two languages simultaneously. I can't even write English with my left hand with the help of my right hand! I am not gifted in the same way intellectually that President Garfield was.

On May 25, 1935, Jesse Owens beat or equaled 4 world records all within 45 minutes, including a long jump of 26'8½"—and he got off his sick bed to do it![3] Even if I trained faithfully every day, ate the right foods, and had the right coach, I could never accomplish athletic feats like Jesse Owens. I can't jump 26'8¼" with two jumps! I am not gifted in the same way physically as Jesse Owens was.

We are also different emotionally. Some of us are hyper in temperament. Some of us are more low-keyed like Calvin Coolidge. (Reportedly, when told that he had died, someone responded, "How can they tell?") Others of us are somewhere in between.

We are not all equally endowed. To some, God gives five talents; to some, God gives two talents; and to others, God gives one talent. Diversity in the distribution of talents is a reflection of the purpose of God and not an assignment of value. The five-talent person is not better than the two-talent person or the one-talent person—not better; just different. Value is determined not by what we have but by what we do with what we have.

Success

As construction began on a magnificent cathedral, an angel came and promised a large reward to the person who made the most important contribution to the finished sanctuary. As the building went up, people speculated about who would win the prize. The architect? The contractor? The woodcutter? The artisans skilled in gold, iron, brass, and glass? Perhaps the carpenter assigned to the detailed grillwork near the altar? Because each workman did his best, the complete church was a masterpiece. But when the moment came to announce the winner of the reward, everyone was surprised. It was given to an old, poorly dressed peasant woman. What had she done? Every day she had faithfully carried hay to the ox that pulled the marble for the stonecutter.[4]

What is success in God's eyes? In our day, success means being the biggest and the best. But what does God reward? Notice two insights from the Storyteller.

When we focus on the master's response to the one-talent man, we learn that success is measured by the relationship between what we *are* and what we *were*.

The one-talent man was condemned because he did nothing with his talent. As a result, he was the same when the master returned as he was when the master left. He started with one talent and ended with one talent. There was no difference between what he had been and what he had become. Failure is not failing to match other people's talents, but failing to maximize our own.

When we focus on the master's response to the two-talent man and the five-talent man, we discover that success is measured by the relationship between what we *are* and what we *could be*.

The two-talent man and the five-talent man both received the same commendation from the master because they had developed their potential to the fullest. The two-talent man doubled his, and the five-talent man doubled his. In both cases there was a correlation between their potential and the actuality in their lives. Success is not being *the* best but being *our* best.

Since God made us, God knows what we are capable of doing. God does not hold us accountable for what we cannot do, only for what we can do.

Conclusion

What incredible good news this is! We cannot be the best in most areas because others are more gifted in those areas than we are. But each of us can be our best. We can take our gifts and develop them. We can face our potential and maximize it. We can seize our opportunities and take advantage of them. We can be our best.

Whether we are one-talent people or two-talent people or five-talent people, if we will so live that we are better today than we were yesterday and so that we will someday in the future be the best we can be, then we can hear from the Master the magnificent words of commendation: "Well done, good and faithful servant" (Matt 25:21 NIV).

Notes

[1]Michel Parouty, *Mozart: From Child Prodigy to Tragic Hero* (New York: Harry N. Abrams, 1993) 169.

[2]Richard B. Manchester, *Incredible Facts* (New York: Exeter Books, 1985) 130-31.

[3]Ibid., 187.

[4]Hanz Finzel, *The Top Ten Mistakes Leaders Make* (Wheaton IL: Victor Books, 1994) 35.

You Can Have It All!

Matthew 13:45-46

Bertha Adams was a pitiful case. At 71 years old and weighing only 50 pounds, she begged door-to-door for food and clothed her emaciated body with Salvation Army clothing. On April 5, 1974, she died of malnutrition in West Palm Beach, Florida, after spending the last few days of her life in the hospital. When Bertha died, authorities made a remarkable discovery. Bertha Adams left behind a fortune of more than $1,000,000, including more than $800,000 in cash and several hundred shares of valuable stock she had stored in two safety deposit boxes! She had unlimited resources at her disposal, but she chose to go through life living beneath her privileges.[1]

Many Christians today are like Bertha Adams. With abundant resources available, we choose to live beneath our privileges.

In one of his shortest but most powerful stories, the story of the perfect and priceless pearl, the Storyteller shared the good news that we don't have to be deprived of what God has for us; we can have it all. Even more important, he revealed to us the simple key that will enable us to experience this abundance, both in the here and now and in the then and there.

The story revolves around a pearl merchant and his search for the perfect pearl. He spent a lifetime dealing with pearls of varying degree of value. Then one day he found the perfect pearl. He found the pearl of great price. What did he do? He immediately sold everything he had and bought that one special pearl, because he knew that when he had the one special pearl, he had it all.

The pearl represents the essence of life. Jesus said we can have it, if we are willing to pay the price. What is the price? This pearl merchant "went and sold all that he had" (v. 46). What is the price we must pay to experience the essence of life? According to Jesus, it will cost us everything we are and everything we have.

That's what faith means. We often say, "If we believe in Christ, we can have life," which is certainly true. But we must remember the corollary to this truth: Believing in Christ means taking everything we are and have and putting it under his control. To believe means to lean the whole weight of our lives on Jesus Christ. This is the key to having it all, the cost of the pearl of great price. It demands much more than just an occasional thought of God, infrequent attendance at church, a timid attempt to be a good person, sporadic prayer, or following some religious rituals.

To have it all, we must be willing to give it all, to lean our whole weight on Jesus Christ, to take everything we are and have and put it under his control. This might seem like quite a price to pay, until we fully realize what we receive. We exchange everything we are and everything we have . . . for everything God is and everything God has. That's quite a deal.

When we give up what we are and have in exchange for what God is and has, then we discover, as Jesus said in his story, we can have it all.

In the Here and Now

During the Old West days a father and his son went into town to pick up supplies at the general store. The boy patiently waited as the father found all the things he needed.

As the father was paying the proprietor of the store, the proprietor said to the little boy, "Son, you've been such a good boy. Why don't you stick your hand into this bowl and get all the hard candy you want?"

The boy just stood there, saying nothing and doing nothing. Finally, the proprietor reached his hand into the bowl, grabbed a handful of candy, and put it in the hands of the little boy.

On the way home the father said to his son, "Son, I've never known you to be bashful before. Why didn't you take a handful of candy like the man said?"

*The little boy said, "I knew if I didn't, he would give me
some himself. And his hand is bigger than my hand!"*

Many people go all the way through life without ever getting what
they want, without ever experiencing life. They desire power, but
all they know is impotence and failure. They seek peace, but all
they experience is turmoil and unrest. They search for love, but all
they encounter are temporary relationships. They desire life, but all
they get is a hollow imitation of the real thing. They go through life
and never have in their possession the pearl of great price, the
essence of what living is all about. Why? Because they are not willing to pay the price. They hold on so firmly to what they have that
they miss what God wants to give them.

What keeps us from letting go and letting God?

Sometimes it is *fear*. Fear is one of the most powerful forces at
work in human life—fear of failure, fear of being conned, fear of
having our values taken from us, fear that something will happen
to our children, fear of bankruptcy, fear that life will end before it
even begins. Fear drives almost everything we do. Because we are
afraid we will not like what God has planned for our lives, we hold
on to our lives instead of letting go.

Sometimes *pride* keeps us from receiving God's best. Pride
declares, "I can do it myself. I know what is best for me. I don't
need God's help." Pride causes us to hold on to our thimble full of
blessings instead of lavishing in the ocean of blessings God has for
us. As Calvin Miller put it: "Egotism seldom stops celebrating its
own power long enough to marvel at God's."[2]

Sometimes *busyness* keeps us from having all God intends for
us. Few writers have addressed this issue with such profound
simplicity as has Eugene Peterson. Busyness is often a sign of
importance in today's world. We've transferred this thought pattern
to the church and presented our busyness for God as a sign of our

commitment. Peterson says the word busy is a symptom not of commitment but of betrayal.

> The adjective busy set as a modifier to pastor should sound to our ears like adulterous to characterize a wife or embezzling to describe a banker. It is an outrageous scandal, a blasphemous affront.[3]

We can exchange the word "Christian" for the word "pastor" in Peterson's statement and capture the primary barrier that keeps us from knowing God with such an intimacy that we will experience God's blessings in the here and now. We are so busy carrying out our agenda that we miss out on God's agenda.

If we are willing to let go of everything we have, then our hands will be opened to receive what God has. And we will discover, as did the little boy, that God's hands are bigger than our hands. We can have it all, here and now. We can experience abundant life, if we are willing to pay the price.

In the Then and There

A great king in the West of Ireland named Fergus McDermot O'Donnell ruled over the Kingdom of Kerry. He was a good king who ruled his people justly and wisely. The people called him "Fergus the Good." When he grew old and sickly, and he knew he was going to die, he summoned his people for a final farewell. Then, as life was slipping away, he took a quick glance around at the green hills, the blue skies, the golden fields, and the silver lakes of the land he loved. Just as he commended his soul to God, he scooped up in his right hand a clump of thick, rich turf. The next thing he knew he was at the gates of a big city with ivory walls and a big gold-and-silver gate.

"And who are you?" asked the man sitting at the gate.

"I'm King Fergus McDermot O'Donnell, king of Kerry, and I would like to get into the heavenly city." All the while the king was holding the clump of Kerry turf behind his back.

The gatekeeper punched in some information on his PC, and words filled the screen. *"Yes,"* the man said, *"We've been expecting you."* He punched a button, and the silver-and-gold gates began to swing open.

As the king moved toward the gate, the gatekeeper said, *"Just a minute, your majesty. What's that you're holding in your hand?"*

"Oh, it's nothing," said the king.

"Tis too," said the gatekeeper as he pushed a button to stop the gates. *"What do you have?"*

The king explained, *"It's just a bit of Kerry turf, to remind me of home."*

"Nope," said the gatekeeper. *"You can't have it. It's against the rules. No one enters the kingdom of heaven save with empty hands."*

"If I can't come in with my handful of Kerry turf, I don't want to come in," protested the king.

"Your choice," said the gatekeeper as he closed the doors. *"Rules are rules."*

The gatekeeper picked up the phone and said something, after which he pushed the button to open the gates. Out strode God. God hugged the king and said, *"It's good to see you, Fergus, my boy. We've been waiting for you a long time. Just toss aside that little bit of Kerry turf, and come on in. There will be singing and dancing and telling stories all night long."*

"Sir," said the king, *"I'm not coming in if I can't bring my little handful of Kerry turf."*

The Lord frowned and said, *"Fergus, we can't let you do that. Rules are rules. You can't come into the kingdom of heaven save with empty hands."*

"I can wait," said the king. God went back into the city, and the great silver-and-gold gates clanked shut.

Later, God came back to Fergus, disguised first as an Irish countryman, and then as a little girl similar to King Fergus' granddaughter. Each time when the king was told he had to throw away his handful of Kerry turf to enter heaven, he resolutely refused.

The sun went down, the night got darker and darker, and rain was coming down. King Fergus began to think about his predicament. "What a fool," he said to himself. "This isn't the kingdom of Kerry. This is the kingdom of heaven. They're not going to change the rules for me. I can't sneak in." With a loud sigh, he strolled over to the gatekeeper and said, "Sir, there's no sense fighting the Lord God, is there?" With that, he tossed the handful of turf on the ground.

"Not at all," said the gatekeeper with a smile. He punched in the code, and the big silver-and-gold gates of heaven clanked open. As the king walked through the gates, the gatekeeper said for the umpteenth time: "No one goes through those gates save with empty hands."

When the king walked through the big silver-and-gold gates, do you know what he found inside? Inside, waiting for King Fergus McDermot O'Donnell, were the green hills, the blue skies, the golden fields, the silver lakes, and the whole Kingdom of Kerry! He gave up a handful of turf, and he got the whole thing![4]

For the Christian, the end of life is not the end of LIFE! The eternal life that is ours in Christ is not just life of a different quality; it is also life that never ends. Death is simply the anesthetic God gives us when we exchange the physical body of this world for the spiritual body of the world to come.

Heaven is the word we use to refer to this life after life. Heaven has been a favorite topic of preachers and hymn writers in the past. In the present generation interest in the hereafter has been overshadowed by interest in the here and now. Yet this eternal dimension of the Christian faith remains. Heaven is still our eventual destination as Christians.

Surprisingly, descriptive details about heaven in the Bible are sparse. C. S. Lewis reduced the promises of Scripture concerning heaven to five basic ideas:[5]

• We will be with Christ.
• We will be like Christ.
• We will have "glory."
• We will be fed or feasted or entertained.
• We will have an official position in the universe.

The overall thrust of the biblical description is that heaven will be an experience far greater than we have ever known before.

How can we have all this? What we decide now determines what we experience later. If we are willing to pay the price, if we are willing to let go of everything we have, then our hands will be opened to receive what God has. We will discover, as did the king of Kerry, that we can have it all! We can have it all, then and there. We can experience eternal life, if we are willing to pay the price. The price is everything we are and everything we have. But here's the good news. In exchange for everything we are and have, God offers everything God is and has. What a deal!

Conclusion

In the story of the priceless pearl the Storyteller refutes two falsely held views in our society: (1) easy believism and (2) the Christian faith as a suppression of life.

The call to follow Christ demands something. More accurately, it demands everything. Jesus verbalized this truth in his call to discipleship in Mark's Gospel:

> If any want to become my followers, let them deny themselves and take up their cross and follow me. For whoever wants to save his life will lose it, but whoever loses his life for me and for the gospel will save it. (8:34-35)

The pearl of great price can be ours only at the cost of everything we are and have. No easy believism here!

Giving up everything we are and have to follow Christ does not mean taking a pathway to paucity and despair. Rather, it is entering a pathway to abundance and unparalleled joy. Paul captured this truth in dramatic words in his letter to the Corinthians:

> All things are yours, whether Paul or Apollos or Cephas or the world or life or death or the present or the future—all belong to you, and you belong to Christ, and Christ belongs to God. (1 Cor 3:21-22)

I have spent my lifetime as a Christian trying to comprehend the full dimensions of this promise. Everything belongs to us as Christians—all great teachers (Paul or Apollos or Cephas), all great facts (the world or life or death), all time (the present or the future). Everything belongs to us because we belong to Christ and Christ belongs to God! No paucity here!

Evangelist Sam Jones (1847–1906) was encouraging a man to become a Christian. The man hesitated because of the sacrifice he would have to make in order to follow Christ. "Sacrifice!" Jones retorted. "Fourteen years ago I emptied a whole lot of dirt out of my pockets, and God filled them with diamonds. Think of me going around saying, 'I had to give away a whole lot of dirt for diamonds.' Isn't that a nice thing to give up? Isn't that a sacrifice to make?"[6]

Dirt for diamonds! Everything we have for everything God wants to give us! Wouldn't you like to make that kind of exchange?

Notes

[1]Brian Harbour, *Rising above the Crowd* (Nashville: Broadman, 1988) 10.

[2]Calvin Miller, *The Table of Inwardness* (Downer's Grove IL: InterVarsity Press, 1984) 34.

[3]Eugene H. Peterson, *The Contemplative Pastor* (Grand Rapids: Wm. B. Eeardmans, 1989) 17.

[4]Andrew M. Greeley, *Confessions of a Parish Priest* (New York: Simon and Schuster, 1986) 502-506.

[5]C. S. Lewis, *The Weight of Glory*, vol. 1 (New York: Simon & Schuster, 1975) 31.

[6]*Treasury of Great Gospel Sermons*, vol. 1 (Grand Rapids: Baker Book House, 1949) 103.

Dirty, Rotten Hero

Luke 16:1-9

Ma and Pa Kelly had a very good year in turnips. Pa Kelly hitched up his old horse, Nellie, and went to town to sell the turnips. He sold the turnips for a very good price, much more than he'd ever received before. Pa bought some new clothes for himself—a hat, shoes, socks, shirt, underwear, and a brand new pair of overalls. The salesman put the new clothes in a big box, and Pa Kelly loaded the box in his wagon.

"Giddap, Nellie," he said, starting homeward. "We're gonna surprise Ma when we get home."

Along the road he saw a lake and felt like taking a bath. As he undressed, he looked at the old clothes he'd been wearing for thirty years and threw them into the lake. He wouldn't need them anymore. He swam around for about twenty minutes. When he walked over to the wagon to get his new clothes, he discovered the box was missing. Somebody had stolen the new clothes. He looked all over, but couldn't find them. He got up on the seat of the wagon.

"Come on, Nellie," he said. "We're gonna surprise Ma anyway!"

We can surprise people in many ways. Sometimes we surprise people by what we do, and at other times by what we say. Perhaps nothing Jesus ever said was more surprising than the punch line for his story about the incompetent but ingenious employee.

This employee, who was a manager, was called in by the CEO because of his poor performance. The CEO told him his job was to be terminated. Before the termination, however, the manager adjusted the accounts of several big customers so they would not have to pay as much. He hoped thereby to make friends who would help him after he lost his job.

As Jesus told the story of this unsavory character, the righteous indignation of the disciples undoubtedly rose to a crescendo as they prepared for Jesus to pronounce the condemnation of God on this man. Imagine their surprise when, instead, Jesus commended the man. Jesus called the manager a dirty, rotten . . . hero!

Biblical commentators have gone through gyrations trying to twist this story into something other than what it is. G. Campbell Morgan, for example, makes a rigid distinction between the term "the master" in the story and the master who is telling the story. He concludes that even though the master in the story commended the worker, Jesus had no commendation for the man's action.[1] The editors of the Living Bible paraphrase verse 9 to completely change the meaning of the story. They have Jesus say, "But shall I tell you to act that way, to buy friendship through cheating? Will this ensure your entry into an everlasting home in heaven? No!"

Both G. Campbell Morgan and the Living Bible translators are wrong. The Lord commended the man's action. Jesus suggested to his disciples that they should "act that way." All such attempts to soften Jesus' statement distort the impact of the story. This man was a dirty, rotten hero. And in verse 8 Jesus explained why: "For the children of this age are more shrewd in dealing with their own generation than are the children of light."

Jesus was not commending the dishonesty of "the children of this age." Rather, he was commending a characteristic response to life in the children of this world that he wanted to see in the children of God. This characteristic response can be expressed with two distinct words: determination and intelligence.

Determination

Some years ago President Jimmy Carter addressed several thousand persons at a convention. When he was in the armed services, President Carter said, he was committed 100% to being a good officer. When he began his climb toward the presidency, he did it with the same enthusiastic commitment. He was 100% committed to winning the election, and so was every member of his family. After a brief pause, he added, "But I have never been 100% committed in the same way to God's work."

62

Dirty, Rotten Hero

Jimmy Carter's testimony is the testimony of most Christians. Few Christians are members of the 100% committed club. Jesus confronted his disciples with the question: "Why not?" Why not be just as enthusiastic toward and just as determined about extending the kingdom of God as we are in savoring the pleasures of this world? Why not be willing to spend time to accomplish something for God? Why not be determined to communicate God's word to the world?

To succeed in business, we get up early and go to bed late, face every obstacle with optimism, burn the candle at both ends, and sometimes even ruin our health and destroy our family. To produce a beautiful lawn, we spend hundreds of dollars and hundreds of hours in sweat and toil. To succeed in a sport, we buy all the right equipment, purchase the proper uniform, spare no expense on lessons, and keep on trying, despite our feeble assault at success. Enthusiasm, persistence, determination—these words describe our actions as we pursue our goals in the world.

When we switch to the realm of religion, however, we display a different approach. We don't want to appear too enthusiastic about the cause of Christ for fear someone will describe us as a fanatic. We don't want to appear too definite about our beliefs for fear someone will call us dogmatic. We don't want to appear too determined about our task for fear someone will call us pushy. If we could revise the words of the old hymn, we would sing:

> Sit down, oh men of God,
> You cannot do a thing.
> When it is pleasing to God's will,
> His kingdom He will bring.

Two thousand years ago Jesus held up a mirror in which he wanted his disciples of all ages to see their insipid, unenthused, halfhearted dullness. He wanted us to realize this is not the way it should be in the kingdom of God.

Someone has suggested we need an alarm clock to ring when it is time to rise to the occasion. That time is now. We are doing God's work. We are part of God's family. We are proclaiming God's word. We are headed for God's eternity. We need to get excited about it. We need to show the same enthusiasm, the same excitement, the same determination for the things of God that we do for the things of the world.

Intelligence

A farmer was sentenced to prison for robbing a bank. His wife, still on the farm, was faced with the responsibility of planting the potato crop. She sent a note to her husband in prison, saying, "Do you think I am going to dig up the field and plant the potatoes myself?"

The farmer sent an immediate reply: "Whatever you do, don't dig up the field. That's where the money is hidden."

A week later his wife wrote back: "Somebody must be reading your mail. Some men came and dug up the field. What should I do now?"

"Plant the potatoes," he replied.

The dirty, rotten hero in the story was intelligent in his own right. Granted, he had caused his own problem. Granted, he was an unsavory character. He nevertheless reacted to his problem in an intelligent way. He used his head.

The word in verse 8 translated "shrewdly" comes from the root word that refers to the mind or the discerning intellect. Jesus used this word to explain how worldly people display more intelligence in pursuing their goals than Christians do in pursuing spiritual goals.

This soon-to-be-unemployed manager did not spend time feeling sorry for himself. He did not try to place the blame for his problem elsewhere. He did not become bitter. He did not give up. Rather, he set his mind to work. He activated his brain with the question, "What can I do about it?" He considered his alternatives, and then acted with intelligence. At times it is possible to be too smart for our own good. On most occasions, however, we do not use the brains God has given us to act intelligently when we are doing God's work.

The man in Jesus' story was dirty and rotten, but he was nevertheless a hero, because he used his head. Look at verse 4. The Greek word there is like a burst of daylight in the darkness, like the exuberant exclamation of discovery. "I've got it," he said as a light clicked on in his mind. He thought it through until he knew what to do, and then he acted.

We need people to face the challenges in the spiritual realm with the same kind of imagination and level of intelligence. We need Christian men and women who will show as much intelligent imagination in doing the work of the kingdom as they do in their own business. We need determined, thinking disciples.

Conclusion

John Wesley, the dynamic leader who founded the Methodist church, was preaching to a crowd one day. In his sermon he explained the meaning of a certain Greek word. Someone from the audience interrupted Wesley with the statement, "God don't need your learning." Without missing a beat, Wesley retorted, "God doesn't need your ignorance either!"[2]

God does not need Christians who apply their intellect and demonstrate their determination when seeking personal goals and then tackle the tasks of the kingdom in an empty-headed, halfhearted way. God wants Christians who will think! God needs Christians who are passionate about the work of the kingdom.

Notes

[1]G. Campbell Morgan, *The Parables and Metaphors of Our Lord* (Old Tappan NJ: Fleming H. Revell, 1943) 218.

[2]Fulton J. Sheen, *Treasure in Clay* (Garden City NY: Image Books, 1980) 300.

It's Party Time

Mark 2:18-20

At a very old age, with his health almost gone and his eyesight failing, Patrick of Ireland was to baptize a pagan king who had recently become a Christian. In the early morning Patrick led the new convert into the river. Patrick took into the water an iron standard formed as a cross to signify in whose name the baptism was being performed.

Because of his poor eyesight, when he thrust the standard into the bottom of the river, he put the sharpened point through the foot of the king who was being baptized. The king did not react, and it was only after Saint Patrick saw the crimson in the water that he realized what he had done.

Sorrowfully, he said to the young king, "My son, why did you not cry out?"

The king responded, "Why should I cry out, Father? I thought it was part of the baptism."

Many people view Christianity as a life of constant demands, endless sacrifices, and unparalleled misery. This tendency to set the Christian faith in the context of restrictions and rules that produce misery and distress is best reflected in monasticism, in which individual Christians withdraw from life to a monastery and bind their lives in all kinds of painful restrictions.

For 40 years Besarion refused to lie down while sleeping. He would catch a few catnaps while standing. He believed he was demonstrating his faith by not giving in to his body's desire for restful sleep. Macarius the Younger sat naked in a swamp for 6 months until mosquito bites shredded his skin. Every bite he considered to be a validation of his faith. Simon Stylites spent 30 years on top of a 60-foot pillar. For this brilliant example of faith he was anointed as a saint in the church. Maron spent 11 years in a hollowed-out tree trunk. Every night of misery made him feel more saintly.

These are the extremes to which some have gone when driven by the understanding of faith as a negative, restrictive call to pain.

That understanding of Christianity is common today. The famous description of Puritanism as "the haunting fear that someone somewhere may be happy" can be applied to many Christian groups today. We need to hear another note. Life in the kingdom of God is like going to a party! That was the point the Storyteller made in his little-known story about the courtier and his confused companions.

Let me set the context of the story. Jesus shared a meal with his new disciple Levi and Levi's friends, revealing a life punctuated with joyfulness instead of solemnity. He was doing what a good religious person would not do. He was associating with folks with whom a good religious person would not associate. In shocked curiosity, someone asked him the question: "Why do John's disciples and . . . the Pharisees fast, but your disciples do not fast?" (v. 18).

In answer to the question, Jesus gave three short parables that appear together in each synoptic Gospel. The parables in verses 21-22 about the old and new piece of cloth and the old wine in new wineskins are familiar to most people who have studied the Bible. But the first of the trilogy, the parable of the bridegroom and his friends (vv. 19-20), has often been neglected. In this story Jesus reminded his disciples that a wedding is not a time for gloom and doom, but for joy.

What does the story mean? Jesus reminds us that becoming a part of the kingdom of God and living the life of a Christian are like going to a party. Jesus called for a spirit different from the regimentation and solemnity that characterized the religion of the Pharisees; he called for a spirit characterized by joy.

What is the source of this joy? Is it because we will never have to suffer? Is it because we always get exactly what we want? Is it because we never have to overcome any obstacles? No, joy comes from a recognition of the unparalleled benefits that are ours as Christians. Why is being a Christian like going to a party?

Pardon

The trial had been going for several days when the defendant interrupted the trial by standing up and announcing to the judge, "Your honor, I wish to change my plea to guilty."

"Why didn't you do so at the beginning of the trial?" the judge demanded to know.

"I thought I was innocent," explained the accused, "but at that time I hadn't heard all the evidence against me."

When all the evidence is presented against us, we must admit that we are not innocent. Sometimes we don't even have to hear all the evidence against us. We just know in our hearts that we are guilty.

All of us have been there. All of us are aware of our sin. All of us are conscious of our guilt. What can we do about our sin? How can we find relief from this burden of guilt? An answer is available for those who are a part of the kingdom of God. Jesus said, "Truly I tell you, people will be forgiven for their sins and whatever blasphemies they utter" (Mark 3:28). When we turn to Jesus in confession and repentance, our sins are forgiven.

Talk about happy! Knowing that we don't have to carry our guilt any longer brings joy to the Christian. Our joy grows out of the knowledge that we have a pardon from God.

Purpose

Arkansas State and Texas A & M played a crucial football game a number of years ago. Bear Bryant coached A & M at the time. The Aggies, featuring Heisman Trophy winner John David Crow, were the number one team in the nation and thus were big favorites to defeat Arkansas. However, in the last quarter the Aggies led by only one point, 7-6. The Aggies had the ball and were moving in for a touchdown and running out the clock.

Suddenly, instead of sending John David Crow through the line, the quarterback, Roddy Osborne, threw a pass. The Arkansas cornerback, Donald Horton, intercepted the ball and started down the sideline toward the goal line for what would be the go-ahead and probably the winning touchdown. He was one of the fastest men on the field. Quarterback Roddy Osborne was not known for his speed. Roddy somehow caught up with the speeding Razorback, tackled him on the 7-yard line, prevented the touchdown, and saved the game.

After the game the sportswriters asked Roddy how he did it. How could a slow quarterback like him catch one of the fastest of the Razorback defensive backs? With a glance toward Coach Bear Bryant, Roddy said, "Horton was just running for a touchdown. I was running for my life!" [2]

We are on this earth for a purpose. Discovering that purpose will give direction, desire, and drive into our lives. Where can we find a purpose worth living for? An answer is available for those who are a part of the kingdom of God. Paul wrote to the Corinthians,

> Now there are varieties of gifts, but the same Spirit; and there are varieties of services, but the same Lord; and there are varieties of activities, but it is the same God who activates all of them in everyone. (1 Cor 12:4-6)

God has a plan. When we become Christians, we become a part of that plan.

Talk about happy! Knowing that in the living of these days we are a part of something that is as all-encompassing as eternity, yet so individualized that our part is uniquely significant, brings joy to the Christian. Our joy grows out of the knowledge that we have a purpose.

Presence

A number of years ago Israel's Prime Minister Begin visited in Washington with Secretary of State Alexander Haig. Begin noticed three colored phones on General Haig's desk. When he asked about them, Haig answered, "The white one goes to the Pentagon. The red one goes to the President's office. The blue one goes to God."

"Do you mind," the Prime Minister asked, "if I use the blue phone for a moment?" Mr. Begin had a short chat on the blue phone with God.

When he completed the call, Haig said, "That was a toll call, Mr. Begin, and the charge is $250."

A month later General Haig was in Begin's office in Jerusalem. Noticing a blue phone on his desk, he asked if he could use it. He picked up the phone and sure enough he was talking with God. After a few moments, he hung up. "How much is the charge?" Haig inquired.

"That will be forty cents," Begin explained.

"Forty cents?" said the surprised Haig. "In our country, it is $250."

"I know," smiled Begin, "but over here it's a local call!"

Wouldn't it be nice to live so close to God that we could get in touch with Him with just a local call? It is the recognition of God's presence in our lives that distinguishes the believer from the nonbeliever. How can we experience the presence of God in our lives? An answer is available for those who are a part of the kingdom of God. Jesus told his disciples, "It is to your advantage that I go away . . . but if I go, I will send him [the Helper] to you" (John 16:7). As someone said it, life is not a solo but a duet. There is a "buddy system" in the universe for those who are in the kingdom of God.

Talk about happy! Knowing that no matter where we go or what we do, the Holy Spirit is with us to give us strength and stability and sustenance—that's what brings joy to the Christian. Our joy grows out of the knowledge that we can experience God's presence.

Permanence

George Beverly Shea once told his audience that one of the occupational hazards of being a well-known gospel singer is receiving songs written by amateur musicians. One song writer sent him an original composition entitled, "God's Grip Don't Slip!" That was probably not much of a song, but what a title.

When I turned fifty, I began to experience some of the signs of aging. My body does not look or feel like it used to. My hair is thinning and turning gray. My mind often makes contracts my body cannot execute. Close friends have died. I have begun to measure my life in terms of how many years until retirement. And I have begun to wonder what the future holds.

Where can we find certainty about the future? An answer is available to those who are a part of the kingdom of God. The writer of Revelation envisioned a day in the future when "the kingdom of the world has become the kingdom of our Lord and of his Messiah, and he will reign forever and ever" (11:15). When that day comes, we will share his victory.

Church buildings are erected and then decay; church leaders come to the forefront only to be replaced by the saints of the next age; church programs are produced that soon give way to newer programs; but the kingdom of God will last forever.

Talk about happy! Knowing that we are a part of something whose end will never come—that's what makes a Christian happy. Our joy grows out of the assurance of our permanence. That's why

Jesus said that being in the kingdom of God is like going to a wedding. The thrill of having an everlasting relationship with the One who controls the whole world is the most joyful experience in life.

Conclusion

Two misconceptions prevent us as Christians from experiencing real joy in life. One concerns the belief that we are not supposed to be joyful, that too much joy reflects a lack of spirituality in our lives. The other misconception has to do with how we can experience joy.

Jesus wants us to experience joy in life. In one of his encounters with the Pharisees a point of conflict was the joyfulness of Jesus' life. Someone asked him, "How is it that we and the Pharisees fast, but your disciples do not fast?" Jesus answered: "There will be a time for fasting and sorrow, but now is the time for joy and celebration" (Matt 9:14-15, author's paraphrase).

As Jesus talked with his disciples on the last night of his life, the circumstances were dire. A dark cloud of uncertainty shrouded them. Yet, into that uncertainty came the declaration of Jesus: "I have said these things to you so that my joy may be in you, and that your joy may be complete" (John 15:11).

Anyone who reads the New Testament carefully cannot miss the characteristic of joy that permeated the life of Jesus and was exhibited in the lives of the first Christians. Joy is highlighted as the fruit of the Spirit (Gal 5:22).

Having accepted the fact that Jesus wants us to experience joy is only half of the solution. To deal with the other misconception, we need to understand the pathway that leads to joy. Good circumstances do not produce joy in a person's life, nor do bad circumstances prevent a person from experiencing joy. Possessions certainly do not provide joy, to which history certainly attests. Where, then, is joy found? It is found in a proper relationship with

God through Christ, which in turn opens us up to the full experience of his pardon, purpose, presence, and permanence.

How we need to hear again today the invitation of the Storyteller to come to the party!

Notes

[1]Jack B. North, "Traveling Light," *Pulpit Digest* (March-April, 1982): 44.

[2]Barry Switzer, *Bootlegger's Boy* (New York: William Morrow and Company, 1990) 53.

Remember Who's in Charge

Luke 17:7-10

One of the most grueling processes in the deserts of the Middle East is the training of Arabian horses. The goal for trainers is to have absolute obedience from the horses. After weeks of demanding discipline, trainers have a final test to see if the horses are ready. They force the horses to do without water for awhile. Then they let the horses loose within sight of water. Just as the horses reach the water's edge and are poised to lunge into the water, the trainers blow a whistle. Some of the horses dive into the water anyway. Others of them stand quivering on the bank, desperately desiring the water, but absolutely obedient to their master. The latter horses are considered trained and ready for service because they know who's in charge.[1]

Christians need to learn who's in charge. In our day of easy believism and convenient commitment we need to remind ourselves that God is in charge and that we have been called to serve God. This was the intent of the Storyteller as he shared with his disciples the story of the rigid and resolute ruler. Perhaps in no other parable was Jesus as severe as he was in this one.

Suppose you have a servant who has just come in from the field, Jesus said. How would you respond to him? Would you ask him to sit down so you could serve him? Would you thank him lavishly for all he has done for you? No, Jesus responded. You would sit down, and he would serve you. And whatever he did, you would not thank him for it, because he only did what was expected of him.

The story presents two parallel principles: it is the place of a ruler to rule, and it is the place of a servant to serve! The ruler represents God. The servant represents us. Here's the point. In our relationship with God, God is the master, and we are the servants. God is not under obligation to serve us. Instead, we are under obligation to serve God. God is in charge. God is sovereign!

The names of God in the Old Testament testify to God's sovereignty. *Elohim*, meaning "to be strong" or "to be in front of," is commonly used. *El Elyon*, "God most high," was used for God in the encounter between Abraham and Melchizedek (Gen 14). Melchizedek was a priest of El Elyon. He met Abraham after his battle. Abraham paid a tithe to Melchizedek and then issued a statement of faith about God. *El Shaddai*, or "the God of the mountain," was frequently employed during the patriarchal period, for example, in Genesis 17:1 when Abraham and his God made a covenant. *El Olam*, "God the everlasting one," is used in connection with the sanctuary at Beersheba (Gen 21:33). Even the name *Yahweh*, the covenant name for God, carries the same impact. It means "I am what I am," or "I will bring to pass what I will bring to pass." Yahweh inspired feelings of confidence and assurance in the lives of the people of Israel, for Yahweh was the God who had made covenant with them.

The Bible confirms the sovereignty of God. The Psalmist declared the sovereignty of God when he wrote, "The earth is the Lord's and all that is in it, the world, and those who live in it" (24:1). Isaiah the prophet sounded the same note when he spoke these words from his God: "Thus says the Lord, the King of Israel . . . . I am the first and I am the last; besides me there is no god" (44:6). The great multitude of saints in the book of Revelation sang about the sovereignty of God as they cried out, "Hallelujah! For the Lord our God the Almighty reigns" (19:6).

Is the message coming through? The God of the Bible is not a cosmic errand runner at our disposal who comes running every time we ring the bell. God is sovereign and in charge. This tale from the Storyteller reminds us how we are to respond to a sovereign God.

Serve God

Vince Lombardi was one of the most successful and famous coaches in National Football League history, a coach known for his toughness. He was also a father.

His daughter Susan met a young man named Thomas Bickham. Bickham asked Susan to type his term paper, but soon the relationship developed far beyond that. One night they were in the basement of Susan's house, working on a paper, when Coach Lombardi came home.

Susan heard Vince slam the door, so she turned to Thomas and said, "I'd like for you to meet my father. I think it's time." Bickham had never met Lombardi and was actually scared to death of him.

Susan called out, "Daddy, I want you to come down and meet Tom."

A pause and then the voice of Lombardi came down like a clap of thunder: "Tell him to come up here and meet me!" [2]

Lombardi wanted this young man to realize he was not at his beckon call. He wanted him to recognize who was in charge! God is not here to meet our needs; we are here to meet God's needs. Serving God is to take precedence over eating and drinking at God's table. In Jesus' story when the servant came in from the field, the master didn't meet the need of the servant. Instead, the servant was expected to meet the needs of his master (Luke 17:7-8).

Several Greek words are translated "servant" in the New Testament. A *diakonos* was a servant who ministered. A *therapon* was an attendant. An *oiketes* was a house servant. A *misthios* was a hired servant. The word Jesus used in the parable is *doulo,* which literally means "slave." A slave was bound to and found his identity in his master. A slave had one agenda: to find out what his master wanted him to do and then to do it. Jesus' story is a reminder that we are bound to and find our identity in God. Our only agenda is to determine what God wants us to do so we can do it.

We can paraphrase the famous statement made by John F. Kennedy in his inaugural address to say: "Ask not what God can do for you; rather, ask what you can do for God." The desire to serve God grows out of the fact that God is in charge.

Serve God Continually

A man went to an old friend to ask for a loan. He offered no collateral and didn't want to be charged any interest. The friend from whom he was trying to borrow the money suggested their friendship was not close enough to justify such a claim on it. Consequently, he refused to make the loan.

"How can you say that?" his friend protested. "We grew up together. I helped you make it through school. I even saved you from drowning once. I helped you get started in business. I persuaded my cousin to marry your sister. I can't believe you'd say we are not close enough for you to make me a loan."

The other man replied, "I remember when you did all of that, but what have you done for me lately?"

Our service for God is not just a part-time, temporary assignment. It is the responsibility of a lifetime. We see this in Jesus' story. The servant left his responsibility in the field only to be confronted by his responsibility at the house.

So it is for us. We never escape our responsibility to God. All of life is lived under a certain sense of oughtness. We can never say: "For an hour, I am not under obligation to God"; or "For the weekend, I am not under obligation to God"; or "Now that I have completed that task, I am going to take a sabbatical from my responsibility to God."

No! Serving the Father is lifetime employment for the child of God. There is no retirement. In good times or in bad, in sickness or in health, in youth or in old age, we are never released from our responsibility to serve God. We must serve God continually.

Serve God Contentedly

Wilfred Greenfell (1865–1940), an English doctor and missionary, spent his lifetime serving and witnessing to the people of Labrador. Before he retired in 1935, he had founded 5 hospitals, 7 nursing stations, 3 orphanage boarding schools, and an institute for seamen. In addition, he left behind hundreds of converts. On one of his fund-raising trips back home, he was speaking to a group of Christians about the hardships and struggles he had endured in his service for Christ. Afterwards, a woman expressed her sympathy for all he had gone through. Immediately, he broke into her soliloquy with the remark, "Oh, you completely misunderstood me. I was having the time of my life!" [3]

We should serve God, focusing not on the sacrifices we make, but on the blessings we receive for doing what is expected of us as servants of God. Jesus declared, "So you also, when you have done all that you were commanded to do, say, 'We are worthless slaves; we have done only what we ought to have done' " (v. 10).

It is not enough simply to serve God or to serve God faithfully. We must also serve God with the right spirit, with the proper attitude. I'm talking about the difference between "get to" and "got to." Think about the times you use "get to." I "get to" go to the movie, go on vacation, go fishing, go to the ball game . . . Now think about the times you use "got to." I've "got to" go to work, pay taxes, go to the dentist, wash clothes . . .

There is a world of difference between "get to" and "got to." We need to speak of serving God as something we "get to do" instead of something we've "got to do." Only then will we adequately express our commitment. We are not only to serve God. We are not only to serve God continually. We are also to serve God contentedly.

Conclusion

When James and John sought the favored positions at the right and left sides of the Master, the other disciples were indignant, perhaps because of the presumption of James and John, or perhaps because they felt they themselves should have the places of preeminence. Jesus used this conflict as an opportunity to teach his disciples about greatness and service (Mark 10:35-45). Jesus set side by side two understandings of greatness, that of the world and that in the kingdom of God.

How is greatness measured in the world? Power, authority, control—these words describe greatness in the world. The more people you can control, the more people over whom you have authority; the more power you have, the greater you are. The fact that James and John wanted to be seated in positions of power where they could control others—and the indignant response of the other disciples—revealed that they were all tainted by the world's way of thinking. How is greatness measured in the kingdom of God? By our service, Jesus declared. "Whoever wishes to be first among you must be slave of all" (Mark 10:44).

The battle continues today between these two understandings of greatness. As it was for the first disciples, so it is for us today: the line between these two is often blurred, and men and women of the kingdom succumb to the world's understanding. Therefore, we need to hear again the Storyteller's reminder that we are not in charge; God is. And because God is in charge, we are to be God's servants, serving faithfully and with the right attitude.

In the words of Helen Steiner Rice, "If we approach our civilization with the idea of selecting the greatest word in it, . . . one word naturally arises above all the other thousands and stands out supreme. . . . The Word is Service!"[4]

Notes

[1]Barbara Brokhoff, "God's Pass/Fail Exam," *Pulpit Digest* (September-October, 1982): 37.

[2]Jim Tunney, *Impartial Judgment* (New York: Franklin Watts, 1988) 116.

[3]John N. Gladstone, "The Good Medicine of Cheerfulness," *Pulpit Digest* (January-February, 1984): 23.

[4]Ronald Pollitt and Virginia Wiltse, *Helen Steiner Rice: Ambassador of Sunshine* (Grand Rapids: Fleming H. Revell, 1994) 56.

Cleanliness Is Not
Always Next to Godliness

Matthew 12:43-45

"Two wrongs don't make a right."
"What goes up always comes down!"
"Idle hands are the devil's workshop."
"Everything comes to him who waits."
"Genius is 3% inspiration and 97% perspiration."
"An ounce of prevention is worth a pound of cure."
"If you lie down with dogs, you'll get up with fleas."
"People who live in glass houses should never throw stones."
"Always wear clean underwear; you might be in an accident!"

Our mothers told us things that have stayed with us all our lives. Although we didn't want to hear them at the time they said them, these pieces of advice have turned out to be true. These bits of wisdom are a part of the heritage most of our moms gave us.

Consider another aphorism our mothers probably proposed: "Cleanliness is next to godliness." There is some truth to that old saying, but it is not always true, as we see in the strange story of the stubborn but sociable spirit.

Jesus said, "Picture a person whose house has been cleaned. The unclean spirit that lived in the house is tossed out, but nothing positive is put in its place. The unclean spirit roams around for awhile looking unsuccessfully for a new house to live in. Eventually he goes back to the house from which he was expelled and finds it still vacant. He then gets seven of his sinful sidekicks, and they all move into the house. In the end the house is worse off than it was when only one evil spirit had residence there."

What did Jesus mean with this strange story? The truth can be stated in a single sentence: A negative approach to life is not adequate. Look at the conclusion of the story: "So it will be with this evil generation" (v. 45). Jesus was referring to the Pharisees. This is quite clear as we notice the context of the story. Matthew 12 begins with two incidents on the Sabbath that stirred up the antagonism of the Pharisees.

While passing through a field, Jesus' disciples plucked some grain to eat. According to the negative approach of the Pharisees, this action constituted work and was a defamation of the Sabbath (vv. 1-8). Thus, they criticized the disciples.

When Jesus entered the synagogue, he healed a man with a withered hand. According to the negative approach of the Pharisees this, too, was considered work and broke the laws of the Sabbath (vv. 9-13). Consequently, they criticized Jesus.

Anything done on the Sabbath, even if it was good, was wrong for the Pharisees because they had a negative religion. The roots of this negative approach are found in the Babylonian captivity period. During the Babylonian exile, the Jewish scribes concluded that their defeat came because of the presence of wickedness among the people. When they returned home after the captivity, they determined never to let it happen again. They amplified the law, and then elaborated the amplifications, and then amplified the elaborations until they had a system of a thousand restrictions intended to remove from the presence of the people every hint of evil. The Jews of Jesus' day had a religion of restrictions.

Jesus' story is an indictment of that negative approach to religion. Jesus said, "You have indeed removed every appearance of evil from the lives of the people. But the end result is not righteousness; the end result is emptiness." Their purposeless, joyless, lifeless religion made them worse off than having no religion at all.

Jesus' message is clear: negativism is not an adequate approach to life. Let's apply this simple truth to several dimensions of our lives.

Our Thoughts

A special guest was coming to visit in the home of a family. The mother was very concerned because the guest had an enormously large nose. She was afraid her five-year-old son would say something embarrassing about the man's nose. For two weeks she would say to her son, "Now when he comes, remember not to say anything about his nose."

Finally the day for the visit came. As the guest sat down, the little boy came running through the room. The boy stopped and looked directly at the man's enormously large nose. The mother's heart stopped, but fortunately, the little boy didn't say anything about it. He just waved at the guest and left the room. The mother, relieved that the possible crisis had been averted, turned to her guest and asked, "Would you like sugar or cream with your nose?"

In our thought life the negative approach is inadequate. Saying "I will not think about that anymore" is a guarantee that our attention will be focused on it.

Does telling yourself not to think about food keep you from savoring thoughts about your favorite dish? Does telling yourself not to think about a girlfriend who has dropped you keep you from thinking about her? No! The very statement of what you will not think about plants that thought in your mind. Negative thinking is nevertheless thinking!

How, then, do we get negative thoughts out of our minds? We remove negative thoughts by replacing them with positive thoughts. This is why Paul wrote to the Philippian Christians,

Whatever is true, whatever is honorable, whatever is just, whatever is pure, whatever is pleasing, whatever is commendable, if there is any excellence and if there is anything worthy of praise, think about these things. (Phil 4:8)

When we focus our minds on positive thoughts, we soon discover that the evil thoughts are gone. But if we focus on the evil thoughts we don't want to have, we are doomed to failure. In the area of our thoughts, the negative approach will never do.

Our Morals

Johnny Taurus made an appointment with a doctor because of severe pain in his abdominal area. The doctor's examination revealed an ulcer. The doctor asked Johnny if he had some undue stress in his life that might be the cause of this ulcer.

Johnny, who was married, was silent for a moment. Finally, he confessed to the doctor that he had a girlfriend in a town about 50 miles from where he lived. Twice a week he would drive his old pickup truck to see her. Since the pickup frequently broke down, he often returned late, and he had to devise increasingly more ingenious stories each time to tell his wife.

The doctor, who was a Christian, decided he would scare this young man into a more moral stance. He explained to Johnny that the stress was killing him and that if he didn't remove the cause of his stress, he could possibly die. Johnny nodded to the doctor and assured him he would do something about it.

Six months later Johnny returned for a checkup, completely cured, a new man. The doctor congratulated him and responded that he evidently had removed the cause of his stress. "Yes, I have," Johnny admitted. "I bought a new pickup!"

In the area of our morals, the negative approach is inadequate. Forbidding someone from doing something immoral is not enough to prevent the action. Did prohibition prevent people from drinking? Does the possibility of execution in the electric chair prevent murder from occurring? No! These restrictions only cause more creativity and caution in those who do these things.

At times the restrictions actually stimulate us to do the thing that is restricted. For instance, telling children not to do something is almost a guarantee they will do it. Similarly, a sign that reads,

"Wet Paint, Do Not Touch" often stimulates someone to touch it to see if it really is wet.

How do we get negative actions out of our lives? How do we prevent wrongdoing? We change our actions when we are changed on the inside. Morality is not a matter of outward restrictions; it is a matter of inward renewal. Inward renewal produces true morality, not the force of restrictions from without but the positive propulsion of inward renewal. In the area of morality, negativism is not enough.

Our Relationships

Herman and Henrietta were watching television one night. They had been married for twenty years, but Henrietta was not happy.

Finally, Herman got the clue and said, "Henrietta, what's the matter?"

Henrietta replied, "Herman, you never tell me you love me."

Herman responded, "I told you once, and if I ever change my mind, I'll let you know."

Would your spouse be satisfied if you avoided saying anything wrong by saying nothing? Would your best friend be happy if you avoided doing anything to hurt him by simply not ever being around him? No! Sometimes indifference and neglect are more damaging to relationships than hurtful words or harmful actions. How do we move from the negative to the positive in our relationships?

In his remarkable book *The 7 Habits of Highly Effective People*, Stephen Covey presents the picture of an emotional bank account into which husbands and wives make regular deposits. We all know what a financial bank account is. We make deposits in our accounts and build up reserves from which we can make periodic withdrawals. An emotional bank account is the trust level we build up in our relationship with our spouse from which periodic emotional withdrawals are made. Covey lists six major deposits[1] that build the emotional bank account in marriage:

- continually trying to understand our mate
- attending to the little things in the relationship
- keeping our promises
- clarifying expectations
- displaying an integrity that generates trust
- apologizing sincerely when making a withdrawal from the account

We build meaningful relationships by the positive things we do and say, not from the things we fail to do. In the area of relationships, negativism is not sufficient.

Conclusion

Frederick B. Speakman, a famous preacher from the past, summarized the issue of godliness like this: "And there is a peculiar Christian danger, that you and I get the impression, and in turn, give the impression, that Christianity's big business is to teach us how to say 'No' to temptation. And that isn't its big concern. That is a by-product. Christianity's big concern is to enable us to say 'Yes' to life."[2]

We can say yes to life because of who we are, what God has given us, and where we are going. In the words of Paul to the Romans and Corinthians, and then of Jesus to his disciples:

For you did not receive a spirit of slavery to fall back into fear, but you have received a spirit of adoption When we cry, "Abba, Father!" It is that very Spirit bearing witness with our spirit that we are children of God. (Rom 8:15-16)

Now there are varieties of gifts, but the same Spirit; and there are varieties of services, but the same Lord; and there are varieties of activities, but it is the same God who activates all of them in everyone. To each is given the manifestation of the Spirit for the common good. (1 Cor 12:4-7)

In my Father's house there are many dwelling places. If it were not so, would I have told you that I go to prepare a place for you? And if I go and prepare a place for you, I will come again and will take you to myself, so that where I am, there you may be also. (John 14:2-3)

The Storyteller calls us to move past the negative denial of evil to a positive dedication to good that will motivate us to say "Yes" to life!

Notes

[1]Stephen R. Covey, *The 7 Habits of Highly Effective People* (New York: Simon & Schuster, 1989) 188-98.

[2]Frederick B. Speakman, *The Salty Tang* (Grand Rapids: Fleming H. Revell, 1954) 87.

The Outsider

Matthew 22:11-14

In his autobiography Hank Aaron revealed some of his personal trauma of being an outsider. He recalled memories from his early days in the Negro League. On one occasion the team ate in a restaurant behind Griffith Stadium in Washington. He said he can still hear the kitchen employees breaking all the plates in the kitchen after he and the other players had finished eating to make sure no white person had to eat on the same plate a black person had used. He described the isolation he felt as he broke into the major leagues, the motels in which he could not stay, and the restaurants in which he could not eat. He detailed with passion the death threats and hate mail that came flooding in as he approached and then passed Babe Ruth's home run record.[1]

Through the centuries prejudice has been a divisive factor that has created an "us versus them" mentality. On the basis of age, gender, skin color, nationality, religion, intellectual quotient, or any one of a dozen other factors, the world has been divided into the inner group and those who are considered outsiders.

If you've ever been on the outside looking in, you know the trauma involved in being an outsider. But let me raise this trauma to a more serious level: What would it be like to be an outsider with God? That is the issue at stake in the Storyteller's tale of the visible but villainous visitor.

In Matthew 22:1-10 Jesus told the story of a king who had a wedding feast for his son. Everything was ready, but the guests would not come. Consequently, he sent his servants out into the streets to gather everyone they could find for the wedding feast. The food was laid out; the wedding hall was full; and all the guests were having a wonderful time.

A strange twist is introduced in verse 11. As the king looked over the people at the party, he noticed one guest who did not have on his wedding clothes. This guest was cast into "outer darkness" where there was "weeping and gnashing of teeth" (v. 13).

The king represents God. The party represents the kingdom of God. The guest who was excluded from the party represents those who are outsiders to God. The key issue raised by the story is this: Why was the man expelled from the party? What made him an outsider with God?

Coming to God on Our Own Terms

C. T. Studd was a young, athletic, popular English collegiate who gave his life to Christ and then spent the rest of his life leading others to become Christians. After spending ten years in China, he and his wife returned to England for a time of furlough. He spent the time at home, speaking throughout the country and sharing Christ with everyone he knew.

One night, after a preaching service, he was visiting with his cousin. She had been intrigued by what he said, but had not yet made her decision for Christ. She made a cup of cocoa and took it to C. T. who was sitting on the sofa in the drawing room. He continued to talk, ignoring her while she stood there holding out the cup. She held the cup out toward him again, but still he ignored it.

Finally, she complained, "Why are you being so rude? Why don't you take this cup? It's for you."

C. T. said, "That's exactly how you are treating God who is holding out eternal life to you." [2]

Picture a young man signing up for the army. As he appears for boot camp, he walks up to the sergeant and says, "All right, buddy, I've signed up to be in your army, but this is the way it's going to be. I'm not going to march. I'm not going to pull KP duty. I'm not going to clean my gun. I'm not going to spit-shine my boots. I'm not going to make up my bed so you can bounce a coin on it. And I'm certainly not going to fight. I'm just going to lounge around the PX and read and listen to my radio."

What would happen to that young man? He would be whipped into shape so fast, his head would spin. Yet, we often respond to God in the same way. God holds out the cup of life to us, but we refuse to take it; we want God to come to us on our own terms.

Perhaps that was the problem with the man in the story. In ancient times whenever kings held a party or hosted a wedding, they presented costly dresses or robes to each of the guests. By refusing to wear the garment provided by his host, the guest in the story was displaying a lack of even the most elementary courtesy. He was saying to the king, "I'll come on my terms, not yours."

The lesson of the story is that we come to God on God's terms or not at all. What are God's terms? Jesus spelled it out in his call to discipleship in Mark 8:34. He said, "If any want to become my followers, let them deny themselves and take up their cross and follow me." Three things are involved in following Jesus.

First, we must deny self. Denying self means saying goodbye to self. This does not suggest the kind of self-flagellation that has often characterized Christianity. It simply means saying goodbye to the self that relied on its own strength and lived according to its own purposes.

Second, we must take up our cross. Taking up our cross means accepting whatever sacrifice comes as a result of following Jesus. Many are faithful to Jesus when it is convenient or popular or easy. Jesus called for a commitment to be faithful when it is inconvenient, unpopular, and difficult.

Third, we must follow Jesus. Following means being on the same road as another. The present imperative suggests a continued pattern of following. It means having the same purpose as Jesus. We must be willing to give control of our lives to God. This is the only way we can come to God. These are the only terms on which God will accept us. Perhaps the man in the story was expelled from the party because he wanted to come on his own terms.

Refusing to Identify with God's People

Jimmy Durante was asked to be a part of a show for World War II veterans. He refused at first because of his busy schedule, but finally agreed to do one short monologue if he could immediately leave for the next appointment.

The building was packed for the benefit performance. When Durante went on stage, the crowd was thrilled. He went through his monologue and was greeted with tumultuous applause. He did another monologue and then another as the applause grew louder and louder. Finally, after thirty minutes, he left the stage.

The man who had enlisted him met Durante back stage and thanked him for doing a longer performance. Durante said, "If you'll look out on the front row, you'll see why I had to stay."

On the front row were two men, one who had lost his right arm in the war and another who had lost his left arm in the war, standing beside each other clapping with each of their hands, doing together what neither could have done alone.[3]

The people of God come together, each with our handicaps, each with our limitations, but together we are able to do what alone we cannot do. Maybe the wedding guest in the story wanted to stand alone. He did not want to identify with the other guests at the party. We cannot love God without loving God's people. We cannot identify with God without identifying with God's people.

Every description of the church in the New Testament emphasizes our interrelatedness with each other as Christians. The family of God (Mark 3:33-35) depicts a group of people—mother and father and brothers and sisters—who live in relationship with each other. The *koinonia* (1 John 1:3) suggests people working in unity and partnership with each other. The flock (Acts 20:28) portrays a group of sheep who are together under the protection and direction of a loving shepherd. *Ecclesia* (Matt 16:18) implies a group of people who have been called out and brought together. The body of Christ (Col 1:24) pictures many parts connected to each other and working together under the direction of the head.

There is no such thing as a Lone Ranger Christian. Just as an arm cannot live in isolation from the body, so a Christian cannot function isolated or separated from the body of Christ, which is the church. When we accept God, we must accept God's people, for they go together. Perhaps the man in the story was expelled from the party because he refused to identify with the other guests at the party.

Conclusion

The Christian life includes the vertical dimension and the horizontal dimension, our relationship with God and our relationships with other people. Jesus confirmed these two arenas of life in his answer to the lawyer who posed the question, "Which commandment in the law is the greatest?" Jesus replied:

> "You shall love the Lord your God with all your heart, and with all your soul, and with all your mind." This is the greatest and first commandment. And a second is like it: "You shall love your neighbor as yourself." (Matt 22:37-39)

In both dimensions a demand is placed on the believer—a demand to love. An exclusive love for God—we must love God with all our heart, soul, and mind—leads to an inclusive love toward others—we must love others as we love ourselves.

If we are willing to come to God on God's terms, and if we are willing to identify with God's people, then we can experience the joy of being a part of the forever family. If we refuse, then we, like the man in the story of the wedding feast, will suffer the unparalleled misfortune of being an outsider with God.

Notes

[1]Hank Aaron, *I Had a Hammer* (New York: HarperCollins, 1991) 34, 245-58.

[2]Norman P. Grubb, *C. T. Studd: Cricketer and Pioneer* (Ft. Washington PA: Christian Literature Crusade, 1933) 99.

[3]Tim Hansel, *Holy Sweat* (Dallas: Word, 1987) 104-105.

God Is at Work

Mark 4:26-29

Jethro went to the big city for the weekend. Since Jethro was from Gunners Junction, everything in the city was an eye-opening, mind-expanding experience to him.

On Sunday morning he went to church. It was over-whelming. He'd never seen such a church. He'd never witnessed such a choir. He'd never heard such a preacher. He'd never been in such a crowd of worshipers. As it turned out, his experience at church was the highlight of the weekend.

When he returned home, he prayed a prayer of thanksgiving for his wonderful weekend. In his prayer he began to talk about the worship service. "Oh, God," he prayed, "it was amazing. It was the most beautiful building I've ever been in. And the choir—it was incredible! And the preacher was so intelligent. And the crowd was so full of excitement. It was wonderful. We just had such great blessings. O, Lord, you shoulda been there!"

The good news is that the Lord is here and at work. One of the most intriguing expressions of this truth was given by the Storyteller early in his ministry. It is the story of the forbearing but faithful farmer.

The farmer plants his seed, and then it grows. He doesn't understand how it happens, nor does he make it happen. It just happens. The seed becomes a blade, and the blade develops a head, and the head produces mature grain. Then the farmer harvests his crop.

What does this story mean? A surface appraisal might lead to the conclusion that Jesus was encouraging indolence or indifference, that Jesus was saying, "Just plant the seed, and don't worry about it. It will all work out okay."

A deeper look reveals another insight. The story is not really about a farmer who plants a seed and watches it grow and then brings in the harvest. Rather, it is about the one who is working behind the scenes to produce the growth. This is not a story about how we work; it's a story about how God works.

This simple story suggests that God is at work in our world. If we can buy into this truth, we will have some ammunition against two of the primary obstacles to productive Christian living: discouragement and impatience.

Don't Despair

A man was standing on the edge of a bridge one day, ready to jump, when a passing motorist stopped to reason with him. "Don't jump," the helper said. "Let's talk about it. Surely, it can't be that bad." They talked for about fifteen minutes, and then both of them jumped off the bridge!

We've all been there! At times the external pressures are so heavy, we feel as if we will collapse. On other occasions we feel, as Harry Emerson Fosdick once put it, that "what we pull ourselves together with is broken."[1] When we come to those places in life when we are ready to give up on life and ourselves, we need to hear again the lesson of this story.

God is at work, so don't despair. God is at work even when we don't understand it. Sometimes God works in mysterious ways to accomplish the divine plan. That's the way it is with the farmer, Jesus said. He scatters seed on the ground and sleeps and rises night and day. Then the seed sprouts and grows, but he doesn't know how (vv. 26-27). The farmer doesn't understand everything about how a seed can die and then, out of that dead seed, life can come. He just understands that God causes it to happen. Likewise, our disappointments can become God's appointments in our lives, for God is at work, even when we don't understand it.

God is also at work when we don't see it. Do you remember the story of Joseph, the fair-haired favorite son of a wealthy patriarch? Joseph lorded it over his brothers and reminded them that, according to his dreams, they would some day bow down before him.

Finally the brothers could no longer endure Joseph. They sold him as a slave to a passing caravan of bedouins. What a turnabout in Joseph's life! Then it got worse.

The wife of Joseph's master became infatuated with him. When he refused her advances, she told her husband that Joseph had tried to rape her! As a result, he was tossed into an Egyptian prison. We don't know how much time passed, but finally Joseph was released from prison, and consequently rose to a position of great authority in Egypt.

A quirk of fate put Joseph in a position to gain revenge on his brothers. They went to Egypt to get food, and Joseph was responsible for distributing the food. At best, he could have refused to give them any food; at worst, he could have thrown them into prison for the rest of their lives. Joseph did neither. Instead, he joyfully accepted them and eventually brought them and their families to Egypt to be with him. The key to the entire episode is found in a statement Joseph made: "And now do not be distressed, or angry with yourselves, because you sold me here; for God sent me before you to preserve life" (Gen 45:5).

Joseph did not recognize the work of God at each step along the way. When he was coughing the dust of the camels as he made his way to Egypt as a slave, he probably cried out, "God, where are you when I really need you?" When he was tossed into prison for refusing the advances of Potiphar's wife, he probably shouted, "This is really great, God. I do right, keep myself clean, and this is what I get for it! What kind of God are you?" As he spent those months in the Egyptian prison, he might have thought of God in terms suggested by H. G. Wells as "an ever-absent help in time of trouble."[2] Joseph didn't see God at work at the time, but later, looking back after years of contemplation, he was able to say to his brothers: "Don't be mad at yourselves. It's okay. God was at work in all of this."

That's the way it is with the farmer and with us. Jesus said, "The earth produces of itself" (Mark 4:28). The farmer doesn't see the plant grow, yet it still happens. Often it is only in retrospect that we recognize the movement of God. Only then can we say about an experience or event in our lives, "God was in it, bringing about God's plan."

The one fixed pole in all the bewildering confusion and uncertainty of life is the faithfulness and dependability of God. Through all the labyrinths of history, the unexpected detours, and the unexplained hurts of our lives runs the thread of God's purpose. God has a plan. And it is slowly, silently, sometimes almost imperceptibly being worked out. God is at work; don't despair.

Don't Panic

To teach her daughter a lesson about nature, Jennie brought home a rose that was not yet opened. She explained to her daughter how a flower grows and how pretty the rose would be when it blossomed. After her nature lesson to her daughter, Jennie went to the kitchen to prepare dinner.

Later, as she passed through the room where the rose was, she noticed that the petals had been torn off and the rose destroyed, prompting Jennie to ask her daughter, "What happened to the rose?"

The daughter responded, "I got tired of waiting, so I blossomed it!"

There are times when we all wonder if God knows what's going on in our world and if God is going to do something about it. At those places in life when we want to take charge and surge ahead of God, we need to hear again the lesson of this story. God is at work; don't panic.

Look again at the last part of verse 28. Jesus described the growth of the seed as "first the stalk, then the head, then the full grain in the head." Growth must go through a certain progression. Instead of trying to pull from the seed the full head of grain, the farmer patiently waits for the process of growth to run its course.

The kingdom of God is like this growth process. God has a plan that is being worked out in history, but there is a certain progression in its unfolding. It cannot be rushed. It moves according to God's timing. We must patiently wait for the process of growth to run its course.

This parable is not an invitation to inactivity, but a warning against furiously surging out on our own and moving ahead of God when we discover how slowly growth in the kingdom proceeds toward its consummation.

"The zeal of many a reformer is disguised atheism," an old quip suggests. Sometimes our impatient activism and furious fanaticism have as their motivation the belief that God is not going to get the job done; therefore, we must do it. Sometimes what God wants is neither activism nor fanaticism, but a relaxed, trustful, waiting as we go about normal activities of our day, knowing that in God's time and way, God will achieve His ends. God has a plan. It is being worked out according to God's pace and timing. God is at work; don't panic.

Conclusion

In a day when many things that happen push our faith to the limits, why should we continue to believe that God has a plan and is working it out? Let me suggest three answers.

Our faith is rooted in the past, in God's incarnation in history in Jesus Christ. To doubt God's work in our world, we would have to deny or discard Jesus. How can we explain Jesus, a man of the first century who still impacts the twentieth century and beyond, a Jewish rabbi from Palestine whose teachings are embraced all over the world, a man who died in bondage but whose death has set us free, a man who claimed to be from God and whose claim was affirmed in his resurrection? The only way I can explain Jesus is to accept what he said about himself: he came from God, and in him God is at work. God's work in the past through Jesus Christ provides a foundation for our faith.

Our faith is rooted in the future, in the promises of God's consummation of history. Even though we cannot always see God's hand in the unfolding of world history, the Bible declares that God's hand is nevertheless there and someday, the writer of Revelation explains, we will say, "The kingdom of the world has become the kingdom of our Lord and of his Messiah, and he will reign forever and ever" (11:15). God's promises for the future provide a foundation for our faith.

Our faith is also rooted in the present, in the numinous experiences that occasionally break into our lives. Sometime during the seventh to ninth centuries, Saint Angus came to a beautiful valley in the Scottish highlands, near Balquhidder. Angus called it "a thin place"—a place where the separation between heaven and earth was very thin.[3] Often we find ourselves in a thin place—like Moses at the burning bush or Jacob at Jabbok or Paul on the Damascus road—when God breaks into our lives and gives a fleeting reminder that He is still at work in our world. These occasional numinous experiences clarify what God has done in the past and give us assurance about what God will do in the future, providing a basis for our faith.

Harry Emerson Fosdick, one of America's outstanding pulpiteers in the first part of the twentieth century, wrote,

> There are two kinds of faith in God. One says if—if all goes well, if life is hopeful, prosperous, and happy, then I will believe in God; the other says though—though the forces of evil triumph, though everything goes wrong and Gethsemane comes and the cross looms, nevertheless, I will believe in God.[4]

Long before Fosdick declared that truth in sermon, the Storyteller expressed it in his tale of the forbearing but faithful farmer. Even when we don't understand it, even when we don't see it, and even when it doesn't fit our timing, God is at work. Don't despair. Don't panic. Have faith.

Notes

[1] Robert Moats Miller, *Harry Emerson Fosdick* (New York: Oxford University Press, 1985) 48.

[2] Paul Powell, *When the Hurt Won't Go Away* (Wheaton IL: Victor Books, 1986) 97.

[3] James W. Cox, *The Minister's Manual* (San Francisco: Jossey-Bass, 1998) 77.

[4] Harry Emerson Fosdick, *A Great Time To Be Alive* (New York: Harper, 1944) 220.

Dealing with Change

Matthew 13:51-52

The world is too big for us. Too much going on, too many crimes, too much violence and excitement. Try as you will, you get behind in the race, in spite of yourself. It's an incessant strain, to keep pace . . . and still, you lose ground. Science empties its discoveries on you so fast that you stagger beneath them in hopeless bewilderment. The political world is news seen so rapidly, you're out of breath trying to keep pace with who's in and who's out. Everything is high pressure. Human nature can't endure much more! [1]

—*Atlantic Journal*
June 16, 1833

This description of life in the early nineteenth century describes life at the end of the twentieth century and also highlights the challenge of each new generation to deal with change. Change has always been a part of human life. It is an undeniable part of life in today's world. Because change is a given, should we resist it at all costs? Or should we accept it unconditionally? How should we respond as Christians?

Gerontolatry

January 31, 1829

Dear President Jackson:

The canal system of this country is being threatened by the spread of a new form of transportation known as "railroads." The federal government must preserve the canals for the following reasons:

One. If canal boats are supplanted by "railroads," serious unemployment will result. Captains, cooks, drivers, hostlers, repairmen, and lock-tenders will be left without means of livelihood, not to mention the numerous farmers now employed in growing hay for the horses.

Two. Boat builders would suffer, and towline, ship, and harness makers would be left destitute.

Three. Canal boats are absolutely essential to the defense of the United States. In the event of the expected trouble with England, the Erie Canal would be the only means by which we could ever move the supplies so vital to waging modern war.

As you may well know, Mr. President, "railroad" carriages are pulled at the enormous speed of fifteen miles per hour by "engines" which, in addition to endangering life and limb of passengers, roar and snort their way through the countryside, setting fire to crops, scaring the livestock, and frightening women and children. The Almighty certainly never intended that people should travel at such breakneck speed.

Martin Van Buren
Governor of New York [2]

Some people resist change unequivocally. They equate new with bad and old with good. They are guilty of what I call "gerontolatry," the worship of the old.

Gerontolatry usually works something like this. When Billy and Betty got married, Betty's first meal was a baked ham. She cut off both ends of the ham, cooked it, and served it to her new husband. He asked her why she cut off both ends of the ham. She answered, "That's the way my mother always did it." The next time he was with his mother-in-law, Billy asked her why she cut off both ends of the ham. She replied, "That's the way my mother did it." At a family reunion, when Betty's grandmother was around, Billy asked her why she cut the ends off the ham. She explained, "That's the only way I could get it to fit in the little pan I had."

Like Betty, many of us are committed to old methods that no longer work, to old truths that no longer apply, to old fears that are no longer relevant, and to old patterns that are no longer necessary—simply because we are convinced the old is superior to the new.

In every generation we have resisted and rejected change in favor of the old patterns and customs with which we are comfortable. How different is the word of the prophet Isaiah: "Do not remember the former things, or consider the things of old. I am about to do a new thing; now it springs forth, do you not perceive it?" (43:18-19). The prophet challenged us to discard gerontolatry and to be open to the new thing God wants to do in our midst.

Neolatry

Joe and John met on the street one day. Joe was very much interested in books, particularly old books. John, on the other hand, was not into "old" books.

John said, "I thought about you the other day, Joe, when I was cleaning out my attic. I threw away this old Bible printed by somebody named Guten-something-or-other."

Joe's eyes got big as saucers. "Not Gutenberg!" Joe gasped. "You threw away one of the first books ever printed. A copy sold at an auction recently for more than $400,000."

John was not too impressed. "My copy wouldn't have brought a nickel," John explained. "Some fellow named Martin Luther had scribbled all over it!"

Just as some persons resist change unequivocally, others accept change indiscriminately. They equate old with bad and new with good. They reject old treasures that are still of monumental value, old people who still have exceptional wisdom, and old methods that still produce superb results, simply because they are convinced that the new is superior to the old. They are guilty of what I call "neolatry," the worship of the new.

Every new generation has rejected custom in favor of new patterns and new methods with which we are comfortable. How different is the word of the prophet Isaiah: "Look to the rock from which you were hewn, and to the quarry from which you were dug" (51:1). The prophet challenged us to reject neolatry and to learn from the timeless wisdom of the past.

The Christian Alternative

Lloyd Douglas, a writer and preacher, often visited a man who was a philosopher by profession but taught violin lessons to pay expenses. His studio was located in the midst of a long row of rooms, all of which housed musicians.

One day Douglas dropped in on his friend and asked, "What's the good news today?"

The old man removed his fiddle from beneath his chin and inquired, "Asked lightly or seriously?"

"Seriously," Douglas responded.

The philosopher stepped to a curiously shaped metal device suspended from a silk cord. He picked up a padded mallet, struck it with a sharp blow, and said, "That is the good news for today. That is an A. It was A all day yesterday. It will be A all day tomorrow, and next week, and a thousand years from now. The soprano next door warbles abominably. The tenor across the hall faults unspeakably. The piano down the hall is out of tune. Noise and confusion all about me. But that is A.[3]

Neither gerontolatry nor neolatry are acceptable options for the Christian. The Christian alternative is described in the concise cameo of the dedicated and dynamic disciple. Jesus said, "Every scribe who has been trained for the kingdom of heaven is the master of a household, who brings out of his treasure what is new and what is old."

The "master of a household" was a servant who had complete authority over the distribution of the goods stored in the treasury. The phrase "what is new and what is old" was a reference to one's Jewish heritage (the old) and the message of Christ (the new). "A disciple of mine," declared Jesus, "is a person who deals with, gains profit from, and shares the benefit of both new and old." Both new and old are important to a follower of Christ.

The Greek word "new" is *kainam*, meaning new in respect to quality. The word refers to something fresh, something with which a person is unaccustomed. The Greek word "old" is *palaia*, referring to something of the past, something with which a person is familiar.

The Christian alternative is neither gerontolatry, an unswerving commitment to the old, nor neolatry, an unquestioned obsession with the new, but instead a balanced approach that recognizes the value of and draws from both old and new. A Christian is neither ashamed of old truth, nor afraid of new truth.

No matter how much nor how fast the world changes, some things will be eternally true, namely, the love of God, the spiritual needs of humans, the value of kindness, and the power of love. God is the same yesterday, today, and forever. To indiscriminately embrace the new and to reject the old is to remove ourselves from the timeless truths that give stability to our lives.

God is the "I Am" who continues to reveal Himself to each new generation and in each new day. Stubbornly holding on to the old and rejecting the new is refusing to allow God to continue to make miracles happen in our lives. Jesus said, "My disciples are to learn from, derive value from, and share the benefit of both the old and the new."

Conclusion

How can we effectively respond to change in our day, avoiding the twin problems of gerontolatry and neolatry? Perhaps Paul's advice to the Philippians in their time of transition during the first century is also a word for each of us in our changing world today.

(1) Bring God into the situation through *prayer.* "Do not worry about anything, but in everything by prayer and supplication with thanksgiving let your requests be made known to God" (Phil 4:6). Even though at times we feel inadequate to confront change, prayer reminds us that God is not inadequate. Anxiety says, "I am not able to deal with all of this change." Thanksgiving says, "Praise God, He is able to deal with this change, because all things are possible with God."

(2) Bring your mind into the situation through *analysis.* "Finally, beloved, whatever is true, whatever is honorable, whatever is just, whatever is pure, whatever is pleasing, whatever is commendable, if there is any excellence and if there is anything worthy of praise, think about these things" (4:8). To think means to calculate as when a carpenter takes careful measurements before beginning a task. After bringing God into the situation through prayer, we need to carefully analyze the changes around us and determine what can be done. We need to bring our minds into it.

(3) Bring your life into the situation through *action.* "Keep on doing the things that you have learned and received and heard and seen in me, and the God of peace will be with you" (4:9). After having sought the mind of God and analyzed the situation, we need to move into action. Writers today refer to praxis, or the practical actions called for by the gospel. As we respond to the changes around us, inspired by the sufficiency of God and driven by our best insights, we will be able to "bring out of his treasure what is new and what is old."

Reinhold Neibuhr's serenity prayer, adopted by Alcoholics Anonymous, is relevant to all of us.

> God, grant me serenity to accept the things that cannot be changed. Grant me the courage to change the things that ought to be changed. Grant me the wisdom to distinguish the one from the other.[4]

Perhaps we could paraphrase Niebuhr's prayer to say, "God grant me the serenity to accept the new. Grant me the courage to acknowledge the old. And grant me the wisdom to discern the value in both."

Notes

[1]Quoted by Charles R. Swindoll, *Rise and Shine* (Portland: Multnomah, 1989) 127-28.

[2]Leith Anderson, *Dying for Change* (Minneapolis: Bethany House Publishers, 1990) 169.

[3]Virginia Douglas Dawson and Betty Douglas Wilson, *The Shape of Sunday* (Boston: Houghton Mifflin Co., 1952) 17.

[4]Clyde E. Fant, Jr. and William M. Pinson, Jr., *20 Centuries of Great Preaching*, vol. 10 (Waco: Word Books, 1971) 348.

Payday Everyday

Matthew 20:1-16

A very wealthy woman died and went to heaven. There she was given a bicycle to ride up and down the golden streets. As she pedaled along one day, she saw her maid go by in a Cadillac and her gardener in a Mercedes. She immediately complained to St. Peter.

"Well," Peter explained, "I have no control over that. The kind of transportation you are assigned in heaven depends on how you lived when you were on earth."

A couple of days later St. Peter saw this same woman pedaling by with a big grin on her face. "What's so funny?" St. Peter asked.

"Yesterday," she explained, "I saw my pastor going by on a pair of roller skates!"

How are we compensated for being followers of Christ? What kind of pay will we receive, and on what basis will it be given? To put it crudely, "What's in it for us?" The Storyteller dealt with this question in a perplexing account of a contractor and his confusing compensation.

The rich young ruler in Matthew 19 refused to make the sacrifice necessary to follow Jesus. Consequently, he missed out on the joys of being a part of the kingdom of heaven. Upon hearing this story, Peter turned to Jesus and asked, "What about us? We've paid the price. We've made the sacrifice. We've left everything and followed you. What's in it for us?" (v. 27, author's paraphrase).

Jesus answered the question with this declaration of the generosity of God: "Everyone who has left houses or brothers or sisters or father or mother or children or farms for my name's sake, will receive a hundredfold, and will inherit eternal life" (v. 29). When we become a part of the kingdom of heaven, God will take care of us because God is generous. Jesus elaborated on this promise in the story about the landowner and laborers.

The landowner needed laborers so, according to the custom of the day, he went to the marketplace and looked over the potential workers. He made his selection, explained the wages, and sent the workers into the field. Three more times during the day the landowner returned to the marketplace and hired more workers, offering to pay them a fair wage. At the end of the day he paid the workers, beginning with those hired at "the eleventh hour." He gave each worker a denarius, the amount he had promised to pay those whom he hired early in the day. Surprisingly, as each group was paid, everyone received a denarius. Those who had worked since the early hours were indignant, calling the landowner unfair. The landowner dismissed them, explaining his action not in terms of unfairness but in terms of generosity. What does this strange story mean?

God Employs Us

Eddie Rickenbacker was born in Columbus, Ohio, in 1890, the third of 8 children. He dropped out of school at the age of 11 to help with the family expenses. He later developed a national reputation as a race car driver and automotive expert. In World War I, Rickenbacker was America's leading Ace. Later he founded Eastern Airlines.

Rickenbacker had a fascination for cars from the beginning of his life. When he was 15, he subscribed to a correspondence home study course on automobiles. For weeks he studied. When he thought he understood enough about cars to do a good job working on them, he walked into the Frayer-Miller Automobile Company of Columbus and told Mr. Frayer, "I want to tell you I'm coming to work here tomorrow morning."

"Oh," Mr. Frayer responded, "and who hired you?"

Rickenbacker replied, "Nobody yet, but I'll be on the job in the morning. If I'm not worth anything, you can fire me."

Early the next morning Rickenbacker returned to the garage. Noticing the floor thick with metal shavings and accumulated dirt and grease, he took a broom and shovel and set to work cleaning the place. He got the job, and the rest is history.[1]

Rickenbacker's kind of audacity might help us get a position in the work world, but it won't work with God. We don't manipulate God. We simply respond to God's invitation. That's what we see in the story of the landowner. He invited the workers to work in the vineyard. The initiative was with him. It was not the laborers who sought him, but he who sought the laborers.

So it is with the kingdom of God. The initiative is always with God. Fourteen different verb forms are employed in the New Testament in reference to the kingdom of God, but not once does the New Testament speak of people building or establishing the kingdom. It is God's alone to establish. For example, in the Gospel of Mark, we find these verbs pertaining to the kingdom: "await" (15:43), "see" (9:1), "receive" (10:15), and "enter" (9:47). Luke refers to "proclaim" the kingdom (9:60).

We do not build the kingdom of God; God does. God's sovereign rule over all the earth is declared, and then God invites us to be a part of it. Only because of God's generosity can we be a part of God's kingdom or God's work on earth.

God Employs Us at Different Times

A middle-aged playboy sauntered up to a young woman in her twenties at a party and presented her with the oft-used line, "Where have you been all my life?" She responded, "The first half of it, I wasn't even born!"

Conflict between old and young has always been with us, but it has become more complicated in recent days. In days gone by, we had only three different age categories: youth, middle age, and "My but you're looking well." Today we have a whole new set of categories.

The "seasoned citizens" are those over age 65, and can be subdivided into a number of other categories. The "boosters," born between 1927 and 1945, are labeled by Tom Sine as "the stabilizing edge of the generational wave of the 90s." The "boomers," born between 1946 and 1964, number nearly 80 million Americans. The "busters," those born after 1964, make up a smaller but very vocal group of 20-something adults. Now there are the "boomlets," the children being produced by the boomers.[2] However we categorize different age groups, and whichever group we fit in, Jesus' story announces an incredible truth.

The landowner invited the workers to work in the vineyard at different hours. The Jewish day lasted from 6 to 6, from sunrise to sunset. So the landowner hired laborers for the vineyard at 6 in the morning, at 9, at 12, at 3, and even at 5 o'clock, when the shadows of sunset were beginning to fall across the land. From the time of Origen (185–254 A.D.), these different hours have been understood by some to symbolize the different stages of human life at which people become Christians.

At the sunrise of life, still haloed by the innocence of childhood, a young child can hear the call of God and begin quietly laboring in the vineyard of the kingdom of heaven. This is the way it was for me. There was no fanfare, no dramatics. My conversion was just the quiet acceptance at the age of 8 of what God had done.

At noonday, when many of life's adventures have already been experienced, a person can suddenly tune in to the channel of God's Spirit and be called to a new life and labor. This is the way it was for the apostle Paul.

At the evening time, when the shadows of life have grown long, at the eleventh hour, even then an individual can become a part of God's kingdom. This is the way it was for the thief on the cross.

It's never too late for someone to become involved in God's kingdom work. Even if we are still standing idle in the marketplace and have yet to join the force of those who are laboring for the kingdom, the generosity of God gives us another chance to say yes to the invitation. God calls people to come into the kingdom at different periods of their lives.

God Determines the Wages

The office came to a screeching halt when the copy machine went down. The boss called a repairman who carefully examined the machine. After a few minutes, he took out a mallet, tapped gently on a screw, and the machine started working again. He handed a bill to the manager for $500.

"That's outrageous," screamed the manager. "All you did was to tap lightly on that one screw. I want an itemized bill."

The repairman scribbled on a piece of paper: "For tapping gently on one screw, $1. For knowing which screw to tap, $499."

Many people complain about what they have to pay employees or about what they earn in the workplace. What wages do we get for our work for God? This is the most intriguing and yet most important part of the story. The landowner first paid the ones who worked only an hour, and he gave them a full day's wage. He did the same to each of the others and even to the ones who had been working from the first hour.

Notice what this symbolic action says about God. The point is not that everyone received the same reward, but that everyone was provided for. The early comers received their reward. They were amply taken care of. Nothing was taken away from them just because the others were paid the same amount. But the latecomers were also cared for. When we labor for God, we will receive all we need. God will never give us less than we are promised. We can depend on God's generosity. No person who ever labors for God will be without reward.

When Rabbi Bun bar Hijja died as a young man in 325 A.D., his former teachers and friends gathered to mourn his loss. Rabbi Z'era, seeking to comfort them, told this parable. A landowner had laborers in the field. One man did so well in the early hours that the landowner took him out of the field to travel with him from field to field. At the end of the day the man who had only worked a short time received the same wages as the others. To the protests of the workers, the landowner replied, "This laborer has done more in two hours than you have done during the whole day."[3]

The different responses of the landowner in the rabbi's parable and Jesus' parable reflect the radically different concept of God that Jesus came to reveal. In the rabbinic version the laborer of two hours worked harder and thus is represented as having fully earned his wages. He was a worthy fellow. The purpose of the rabbinic parable was to extol the excellence of the laborer. In Jesus' version the laborers showed nothing to warrant a claim to a full day's wage. The purpose of Jesus' parable was not to extol the excellence of the laborer but to glory in the generosity of God.

"What's in it for us?" Peter said, "What will we receive for following you and laboring in God's vineyard?" Here is Jesus' answer: "You don't need to be concerned about it. God will take care of you. You will receive your reward. God will treat you better than you deserve. You can count on it because of the generosity of God."

Conclusion

How then should we respond to the generosity of God? We have three alternatives: calculation, comparison, or cheerfulness.

The attitude of calculation develops when we focus on ourselves. When we don't get everything we want, when we are not blessed with the benefits we think we deserve, we complain to God saying, "Lord, I did all these things for you. What have you done for me?" That was the way the workers in the story responded. They calculated the number of hours worked, and thus determined their compensation. Approaching God with a "tit for tat, if . . . then" basis is an unacceptable alternative for Christians. With a calculating spirit, we will never enjoy the generosity of God. God is not a tyrant to bargain with, but a God to serve with a spirit of joy. We don't need to bargain with God. We just need to serve God and trust Him to take care of us.

We can also respond to God's generosity with an attitude of comparison. This attitude comes when we focus on others. When someone receives a blessing, we often begrudge them those blessings because we feel more worthy than they. We question God: "What about me?" we ask God. "Why don't I receive those blessings? Why do I have to live life alone? Why are my children having problems? Why did I lose my job?" The workers in the story responded like this. They compared their compensation for the number of hours they worked with the compensation to the latecomers for the number of hours they worked, and they felt slighted. Approaching God with an "I-want-my-share" attitude is an unacceptable response for the Christian. With a jealous eye, we will never be able to enjoy the goodness of God.

Jesus recommended a more acceptable response to God's generosity: cheerfulness. With this attitude, we focus on God. As early comers in the kingdom of heaven, responding to God with cheerfulness means we will not begrudge the reward given to the latecomers, but instead we will realize that the blessed privilege of walking through all of life with the Father and sharing in His magnificent work is a reward no amount of wages can make up for. As latecomers in the kingdom of heaven, responding to God with cheerfulness means we will not laugh at others because we got off easy, but instead we will regret every hour we spent in idleness, every hour before we found our way through to the meaning of life and to the one who is life itself.

A Sunday School teacher told his group of youth that the pay for being a Christian is not much, but the retirement plan is out of this world! He was at least partially right. The retirement plan for the Christian is out of this world! But the daily wages are not bad either, for God does not pay us on the basis of our works. God pays us out of the resources of grace. Everyday is payday for a child of God.

Notes

[1] "Rickenbacker," *Quote* 78, no. 16 (15 August 1982): 374.

[2] Russell Chandler, *Racing Toward 2001* (Grand Rapids: Zondervan Publishing House, 1992) 36.

[3] Joachim Jeremias, *The Parables of Jesus* (New York: Charles Scribner's Sons, 1963) 138.